101
fun facts about
ANIMALS

A JOURNEY THROUGH THE
ANIMAL WORLD

MARIA PAOLA SETTEMBRINI

Penguins can drink saltwater

Indeed, contrary to what one might think, penguins are able to drink saltwater. These animals live in areas where freshwater is often limited, such as Antarctica or sub-Antarctic islands, where sources of freshwater are scarce.

To maintain their water balance, penguins have developed a unique physiological system. Glands above their eyes, called nasolacrimal glands, filter the salt from the saltwater. In this way, penguins can drink saltwater without causing harm to their bodies.

But this doesn't mean that penguins solely rely on saltwater for hydration. They primarily feed on fish and krill, which absorb freshwater through their diet.

Penguins also have an astonishing ability to retain water within their bodies. They can drink saltwater only when necessary and eliminate excess salt through the glands above their eyes.

Penguins can adapt to prolonged fasting periods, during which they utilize the fat reserves in their bodies as a source of energy and water. This enables them to survive the challenging environmental conditions in which they live.

The ability of penguins to drink saltwater is
made possible by their specialized glands and
water balance system. This capability is an essential adaptation for their survival in environments where freshwater is limited. Nature is remarkable, and penguins are just one of the many
examples of how animals have evolved to adapt
to the challenges they encounter in their natural
habitats.

Chameleons can move their eyes independently from one another

Chameleons are known for their ability to change color and adapt to their surroundings, but their visual system is equally fascinating.

Chameleons have a unique eye structure that allows them to move their eyes independently from one another. This ability is known as "independent eye focusing" and enables chameleons to simultaneously see two objects in different directions.

Furthermore, chameleons' eyes can rotate 180 degrees, which means they can look behind them without turning their bodies. This ability is particularly useful for hunting, as it allows chameleons to spot prey without having to move their entire bodies.

But it's not just the eye structure of chameleons that makes them unique. They can also adjust the shape of their lenses to adapt to different viewing distances. This means that chameleons can see with extreme precision even at long distances.

They can also perceive ultraviolet light, which helps them identify objects and insects more effectively since insects can reflect ultraviolet light differently than other objects.

These small creatures possess a highly specialized visual system that makes them exceptional
animals. Their ability to move their eyes independently and have independent eye focusing
assists them in hunting and survival, while their
capability to adjust the shape of their lenses and
perceive ultraviolet light allows them to see the
world in a more precise and detailed manner.

Koalas do not drink water

Koalas are well-known for their adorable appearance and their diet of eucalyptus leaves, but many people are unaware of their unique habit when it comes to hydration.

In fact, koalas do not drink water in the conventional way like other animals. Instead, they rely entirely on eucalyptus leaves to fulfill their hydration needs. This is because eucalyptus leaves contain enough water to meet the koalas' water requirements and serve as a source of nutrients for these animals.

Eucalyptus leaves also contain certain chemicals that can be toxic to most animals, but koalas have developed a unique digestive system that allows them to metabolize these substances without issues. This means that koalas can survive by eating only eucalyptus leaves without the need for drinking water.

However, koalas still need to intake water on certain occasions, such as during dry seasons or when eucalyptus leaves are not readily available. In such cases, they may drink water from puddles or ponds, or obtain water from wet leaves after rainfall.

Nevertheless, the lack of a conventional water source does not seem to pose a problem for koalas, as they have developed a unique way to fulfill their hydration needs. Furthermore, their dependency on eucalyptus leaves also represents an important connection to the surrounding ecosystem, as they contribute to the dispersal of eucalyptus seeds through their droppings.

Koalas do not drink water like most animals, but they rely entirely on eucalyptus leaves to fulfill their hydration needs. This unique adaptation is an important characteristic of their biology and contributes to their role in the surrounding ecosystem.

Kangaroos can jump up to three times their height

Kangaroos are iconic animals of Australia, known for their incredible ability to jump high and far.

Their jumping ability is due to the structure of their hind legs, which are very strong and muscular. The leg muscles are so powerful that they can store elastic energy as they flex and then release it when they extend, allowing them to leap long distances with relative ease.

The length of a kangaroo's jump depends on its size, but it is estimated that they can jump up to three times their own height. In practice, this means that a kangaroo standing at 2 meters tall can jump up to 6 meters in length. This exceptional jumping ability enables kangaroos to move quickly and with great agility through the habitats they inhabit.

Kangaroos also use their jumps to escape predators, as they can leap unpredictably and to heights that predators cannot reach. This is one of the most effective defense tactics of kangaroos, along with their powerful hind kick that can inflict serious injuries on their adversaries.

They are also known for their unique hopping rhythm. Instead of using both hind legs in synchronized motion, they use one leg at a time to jump, creating a distinctive gait that almost appears like a dance. This unique hopping rhythm is a distinguishing feature of kangaroos and adds to their fascination.

Kangaroos can jump up to three times their height due to their powerful and muscular hind legs. This exceptional jumping ability allows them to move quickly and with agility in their natural environment, as well as defend themselves against predators. Additionally, their unique hopping rhythm makes these animals even more captivating and distinctive.

Lizards can regenerate their tails

Lizards are cold-blooded animals that belong to the reptile family and exist in numerous species worldwide.

One of their most interesting features is the ability to regenerate their tails. If a lizard is attacked or feels threatened, it can choose to detach its tail as a defense mechanism. Once the tail is detached, the lizard can regenerate it.

The process of tail regeneration is incredibly fascinating. The cells in the lizard's tail contain a type of stem cells called blastemal cells, which are capable of dividing and differentiating into new cells that will form a new tail. These blastemal cells are immediately activated after the tail is lost, initiating the regeneration process.

It takes approximately two months for the new tail to be fully regenerated. The new tail consists of muscular and skeletal tissue but lacks some of the characteristics of the original tail, such as pigmentation. Additionally, the new tail may not have the same shape and length as the original tail.

It is important to note that tail regeneration can be stressful for the lizard, and the new tail may not function exactly like the old one. For example, the lizard may have difficulty balancing or coordinating its movements. However, the ability to regenerate tails is still a valuable feature for lizards as it can help them survive in dangerous situations.

Lizards are incredibly fascinating animals that can regenerate their tails. This regeneration process is made possible by the blastemal cells present in the tail, which are activated immediately after the tail loss. Although the new tail may not be perfectly identical to the old one, the ability to regenerate tails is still a very useful feature for the survival of lizards.

Dogs can understand up to 250 human words

Dogs are among the most beloved and appreciated animals in the world, thanks to their intelligence, loyalty, and ability to interact with humans.

According to some scientific studies, dogs can understand up to 250 human words. This means that if a dog is properly trained, it can learn to recognize a wide range of human words and phrases and associate them with specific behaviors or situations.

For example, many dogs are trained to respond to words like "sit," "stay," "come here," "fetch," and many others. In addition to words, dogs can also understand the tones of the human voice and can recognize if a command is given in a gentle or stern manner.

It is important to note that dogs do not understand words in the same way that we humans do. Instead, they can associate words with the behaviors or situations that occur when the words are spoken. For example, if a dog's owner says "fetch" while the dog is running towards a ball, the dog will understand that it needs to grab the ball.

Furthermore, the ability of dogs to understand human words can vary depending on the breed and the individual. Some breeds, such as Border Collies and German Shepherds, are notoriously intelligent and easily trainable, while other breeds may struggle to learn certain commands or words.

Dogs are highly intelligent animals that can understand up to 250 human words when properly trained. This ability to comprehend human words is made possible by their intelligence and their ability to associate words with the behaviors or situations that occur when the words are spoken. If you are a dog lover, know that you can communicate with your four-legged friend in many ways, including words.

Deer can jump over 3 meters in height

Deer are animals that inhabit forests and plains all over the world, known for their elegance and agility in movement.

Among their most impressive abilities is certainly their jumping capability. In fact, deer can jump very high, easily surpassing obstacles that are over 3 meters tall.

This ability is essential for the survival of deer, as they live in areas where there are many obstacles such as branches, bushes, and rivers. Deer must be able to cross these obstacles quickly and efficiently, and jumping is the best way to do it.

Deer can jump so high thanks to their anatomy. Their long and slender body structure makes them agile and swift, and their muscular and long legs provide them with the necessary strength to make such high jumps.

Additionally, deer can rely on their exceptional vision and hearing, which help them detect obstacles and calculate the right distance for the jump.

It is interesting to note that some deer species are capable of even higher jumps than 3 meters. For example, the Andean deer, which lives in mountainous regions of South America, can jump over 4 meters in height.

Deer are incredibly agile and fast animals, capable of jumping obstacles that are even over 3 meters tall. Thanks to their anatomy and exceptional visual and auditory abilities, deer can traverse forests and plains quickly and efficiently, ensuring their survival and success as a species.

Chicks can communicate with their mothers even from inside the egg

Although it may seem incredible, chicks can communicate with their mothers even during their growth inside the eggshell.

This type of communication is possible through the sounds that chicks emit inside the egg, which can be heard by the mothers through the eggshell membrane. The mother responds to these sounds with specific calls, thus helping the chicks develop properly.

This form of communication is crucial for chicks, as mothers can provide important information about the temperature and humidity of the egg, as well as alerting them to any external dangers such as predators.

Furthermore, this early communication between mother and chicks has been shown to be important for their relationship later. Indeed, chicks that communicate more with their mothers during their growth inside the egg tend to have more positive relationships with them even after hatching.

This ability to communicate from inside the egg is not unique to chicks, as it has also been observed in other bird species such as pigeons and pheasants.

Ultimately, the ability of chicks to communicate with their mothers from inside the egg is one of the many wonders of nature. This early form of communication is important for their survival and for building positive relationships with their mothers, and once again demonstrates the incredible ability of animals to adapt and thrive in their natural environment.

Snakes can see through their eyelids

While most animals have two eyelids to protect and moisturize their eyes, snakes have a transparent and movable eyelid called the "ocular scale" that serves to protect and clean their eyes.

But it's not just a simple eyelid, in fact, the snake's ocular scale has another surprising function: it allows them to see even when the outer eyelid is closed. In practice, the ocular scale acts like a lens, able to change shape and position to focus light into the snake's eye.

This ability to see through the eyelids is particularly useful for snakes that hunt at night or in water, where visibility is limited. Furthermore, this feature allows snakes to maintain their focus on a target without constantly opening and closing their eyelids.

In addition to the ocular scale, snakes have another peculiarity regarding their vision: snake eyes are fixed and cannot move like those of humans. Instead, snakes have to move their head and body to look in a different direction. However, this limitation is compensated by their incredible ability to perceive movement.

Snakes are extraordinary animals, and their ability to see through their eyelids is just one of the many astonishing features that make them so fascinating. Their ability to adapt to the surrounding environment and develop innovative survival mechanisms has allowed them to exist for millions of years, continuing to captivate and amaze animal enthusiasts around the world.

Bees can see ultraviolet light

Bees, along with many other insects, have a vision that is very different from ours. Not only do they see things differently, but they can also perceive things that we cannot. One of these things is ultraviolet light.

Bees can see ultraviolet light because they have three types of photoreceptors in their eyes, instead of our two. This means they see the world in a very different way than we do. For example, flowers appear very different to bees than they do to us. Flowers have ultraviolet patterns that bees can see and that are invisible to us. These patterns are particularly important for bees as they are used to find nectar and pollen.

Furthermore, bees also use ultraviolet vision to communicate with each other. For instance, during their waggle dance, bees perform a series of movements to communicate the position of flowers in relation to the sun and the bee colony. This way, bees can share information about food sources with their hive mates.

The ability of bees to see ultraviolet light has also been harnessed by humans. For example, insect traps used for pest control often have colors and patterns that resemble those of the flowers that bees seek. This way, harmful insects are attracted to the traps and can be effectively controlled.

The vision of bees is very different from ours, and they can see things that we cannot. Their ability to see ultraviolet light is an example of how animals can use their senses in surprising and innovative ways to survive and communicate with their environment.

Elephants can remember the faces of people for decades

Elephants are highly intelligent and social animals with extraordinary memory. One of their greatest talents is the ability to remember the faces of people for decades.

Elephants have a brain area dedicated to memory called the hippocampus. This part of the brain is highly developed in elephants and helps them retain long-term information. A study conducted by the scientific journal "PLOS One" demonstrated that elephants can remember the faces of individuals they encountered even after ten years.

Moreover, elephants not only remember faces but also the behaviors and emotions of individuals. They can distinguish between friendly and hostile people, and they can even recognize those who have helped them in the past.

This memory capacity of elephants can also be beneficial for species conservation. For instance, elephants that were captured in the past and later released into the wild can recognize their former caretakers and interact positively with them.

Additionally, elephants can remember the locations of food and water sources, as well as the migration routes of their herds. This memory ability is crucial for their survival in habitats where resources can be scarce.

Elephants are remarkably intelligent animals with exceptional memory. Their ability to remember the faces of people for decades, as well as information about resources and migration routes, is essential for their survival in the wild.

Fish can get drunk

Although it may seem incredible, fish can get drunk. But how is it possible? The answer lies in consuming fermented fruit.

In some parts of the world, such as the Amazon region of South America, certain fish species, like the tambaqui, feed on fallen fruit from trees near rivers. This fruit naturally ferments, producing ethyl alcohol, the same active ingredient found in the alcoholic beverages we consume.

As they eat the fermented fruit, fish become increasingly intoxicated, showing signs of intoxication such as loss of balance and inability to swim properly. This phenomenon can have disastrous consequences for aquatic ecosystems, as it can lead to increased fish mortality and disrupt the balance of the food chain.

Additionally, some fish are known to have high levels of methylmercury, a toxic compound that can cause neurological and cognitive problems in people who ingest it. This means that if these fish feed on fermented fruit containing alcohol, the risk of methylmercury contamination may increase.

While the phenomenon of drunk fish may seem amusing or curious, it is important to remember that it can have serious consequences for both aquatic ecosystems and human health.

Cats can see better in the dark than humans

Cats are known for their keen and adaptable vision, but one of their most remarkable features is their ability to see well in the dark. Cats are known to be nocturnal, primarily active during the dark hours when most animals sleep.

The night vision of cats is made possible by a series of physical and biological adaptations. Firstly, their eyes contain a higher concentration of rods, the light-sensitive cells responsible for perceiving brightness and shape. This means that cats can detect even small amounts of light, allowing them to see well even in low-light conditions.

Additionally, cats have another notable adaptation: the ability to expand their pupils to gather lighter. Cat pupils can dilate up to six times larger than those of their human counterparts, enabling them to gather even the smallest amount of available light.

Cats have a reflective layer of tissue called the tapetum lucidum located behind the retina, which reflects light entering their eyes. This layer increases the amount of light available to the retina, enhancing their night vision.

Thanks to these physical and biological adaptations, cats can see better in the dark compared to humans. This ability is essential for their survival in nature and explains why cats are known to be excellent nocturnal hunters.

Dolphins can sleep with one eye open

Dolphins are known for their intelligence, highly developed communication, and swimming abilities. But did you know that these animals can sleep with one eye open?

Dolphins don't sleep like humans. While we sleep with both eyes closed and our brains go through cycles of light and deep sleep, dolphins sleep by only using half of their brain at a time.

This is made possible by a phenomenon known as "unihemispheric sleep." When one hemisphere of the dolphin's brain enters a state of deep sleep, the other hemisphere remains active and alert, allowing the animal to swim, breathe, and stay vigilant against predators.

This state of unihemispheric sleep enables dolphins to rest for extended periods while still maintaining awareness of their surroundings. That's why dolphins can sleep with one eye open while the other remains closed.

Dolphins do not all sleep at the same time. In groups, they take turns sleeping and keeping watch, so while some individuals are asleep, others are swimming and monitoring the surrounding environment.

The ability of dolphins to sleep with one eye open is a unique feature that allows them to rest safely while remaining vigilant against any potential dangers.

Pigs can be trained to play video games

Did you know that pigs can be trained to play video games? Yes, you read that right! Pigs are not only intelligent and social animals, but they are also capable of learning to play simple video games.

In a study conducted by researchers at Purdue University, a group of pigs was trained to use a joystick to control a cursor on a computer screen. The pigs were then instructed to use the joystick to move the cursor to a specific position, where they would receive a reward.

The trained pigs learned to use the joystick quite quickly, demonstrating a high level of skill and learning. In fact, the pigs were able to complete the task with the same accuracy as some monkeys trained for similar tasks.

This study shows that pigs can learn and adapt to new situations, even though these behaviors do not occur naturally in the wild. However, this does not mean that all pigs are capable of learning to play video games, as there can be individual differences in cognitive abilities among pigs.

Training pigs to play video games is a fascinating example of how animals are capable of learning and adapting to new challenges. It also once again demonstrates the intelligence and complexity of animals, debunking the notion that they are simple creatures driven solely by instinct.

Bats can eat up to a thousand insects in an hour

Bats are nocturnal animals that primarily feed on insects, but some species can also consume fruit, flowers, nectar, and blood. They are among the most skilled mammals in flight, thanks to their wings, which consist of a thin membrane of skin stretched between the fingers of their forelimbs.

But what many people don't know is that bats can consume a tremendous amount of food during the night.

On average, a bat can eat up to one-third of its body weight every night.

This means that a bat weighing around 20 grams can eat up to 6-7 grams of food in a single night. However, there are some bat species that can eat even more: the species known as the Fig-eating Bat, for example, can consume up to three times its body weight in a single night, which means that a single bat can eat up to 60 grams of fruit.

What makes bats so important for the ecosystem is their role as natural predators of nocturnal insects. Some bat species can capture up to a thousand insects in an hour, thus helping to keep the insect population under control. The ability of bats to feed on so many insects is made possible by their sophisticated echolocation system, which allows them to locate flying insects and capture them accurately.

Bats are incredibly skilled animals that play a significant role in the ecosystem as predators of nocturnal insects. Their ability to consume so many insects in an hour makes them valuable allies in agriculture and the prevention of insect-borne diseases.

Butterflies can taste food with their feet

Butterflies, like many other insects, have a taste organ called labial palps, located in their mouth. However, an interesting fact is that butterflies can also taste food through their feet. Yes, you read that right: butterflies have taste buds on their feet.

This happens because a butterfly's sense of taste is distributed throughout its body, including its feet. When a butterfly lands on a flower or another food source, the tactile sensations in its feet allow it to quickly assess the quality and quantity of the available nourishment.

Furthermore, the fact that butterflies have a highly developed sense of taste is evident in how they search for their food. In fact, some butterfly species can fly thousands of kilometers to reach a specific host plant, where they then lay their eggs. They do this because they know that plant will provide the best nourishment for their larvae.

Butterflies are not only beautiful and delicate creatures, but they also have a well-developed sense of taste and smell that helps them find their food and choose the best plants for their life cycle.

Rhinoceroses can weigh up to 4500 pounds

Rhinoceroses are incredibly large and powerful animals. In fact, these mammals can weigh up to 4,500 pounds. There are five species of rhinoceros, but all of them are vulnerable or endangered due to illegal hunting for their rhino horn, which is used in traditional Asian medicine.

Rhinoceroses have thick and wrinkled skin that protects them from scratches and bites. Their skin is also very sensitive and can be used to keep the body cool. When it's hot, rhinoceroses sweat through glands on their skin to regulate body temperature.

Rhinoceroses are solitary and territorial animals. They have a highly developed sense of smell and can detect the scent of other rhinoceroses from long distances. Dominant males will protect their territory and try to drive away rivals.

While rhinoceroses are dangerous animals due to their strength and large size, they are also very vulnerable. Illegal hunting and habitat destruction are the main threats to these magnificent creatures. If we don't take action to protect rhinoceroses and their habitats, we may soon lose these incredible animals forever.

Crocodiles can stay underwater for up to two hours

Crocodiles are among the most feared reptiles in the world due to their power and predatory abilities. But perhaps one of their most astonishing features is their ability to stay underwater for extended periods.

Crocodiles have developed a range of adaptations that allow them to remain submerged for long periods of time, up to two hours. Their skin can absorb oxygen from the water, enabling them to breathe while submerged. Additionally, their lungs can store large amounts of air, allowing them to stay underwater for extended periods without needing to resurface for a breath.

This ability to stay underwater for extended periods is particularly advantageous for crocodiles during hunting. They can remain submerged and surprise their prey from below without being seen or heard, or they can stay motionless for hours and wait for prey to approach.

However, it's important to note that crocodiles are not immune to the dangers of prolonged submersion. If they stay underwater for too long, they can suffer from brain tissue damage due to oxygen deprivation, leading to coordination loss and disorientation when resurfacing. Additionally, a crocodile that remains underwater for too long risks becoming a victim of another aquatic predator, such as sharks.

The ability of crocodiles to stay underwater for extended periods remains an impressive skill and another example of the remarkable adaptability of animals to their environment.

Dogs can hear high-frequency sounds that humans cannot hear

Dogs have a much superior hearing ability compared to humans. They can hear high-frequency sounds that we cannot perceive. Their hearing capacity is also influenced by the shape of their ears, which can efficiently capture sound waves compared to human ears.

In nature, this hearing ability allows dogs to perceive sounds of animals moving in their territory, such as mice, rodents, and other small animals. Additionally, it has been utilized by humans for training dogs as hunting dogs, drug-sniffing dogs, and bomb-sniffing dogs.

However, the hearing capacity of dogs can also be a problem in certain contexts, such as urban environments where there are constant noises, traffic, and other high-frequency sounds that could disturb dogs and make them more nervous. Therefore, it is important to consider the auditory needs of dogs when living with them in urban environments and provide them with a calm and comfortable environment.

Turtles can sense vibrations through the ground

Turtles are fascinating animals that possess many unique abilities, including the ability to sense vibrations through the ground. This ability is particularly useful for land turtles, as they need to detect the presence of predators or other animals to avoid being captured or eaten.

Turtles can sense vibrations through their shell, which is composed of many fused bones. This allows vibrations to travel through the turtle's body and reach its inner ear, which is sensitive to vibrations.

The ability to sense vibrations is especially important for marine turtles, as they need to be able to detect the presence of prey or other turtles through sound. This ability is also crucial for land turtles, as they need to be able to detect dangers and predators through sound and vibrations.

Furthermore, turtles can also sense vibrations caused by the movement of the ground, such as those caused by the passage of a vehicle or a larger animal. This ability is important for land turtles that live near roads or other areas where there is a lot of human activity.

The ability of turtles to sense vibrations through the ground is another one of the many unique abilities that these animals possess, making them incredibly interesting and fascinating.

Cats can jump up to six times their own height

Cats are incredibly agile and flexible animals. One of their most well-known talents is undoubtedly their ability to jump to great heights relative to their size. On average, a domestic cat can jump up to five times its own height. However, there have been cases where cats have surpassed this record and managed to jump up to six times their height!

But how do cats jump so high? Firstly, they can accurately assess the distance and position of their target. Additionally, their muscles possess remarkable strength and speed, allowing them to jump with great power. However, what truly makes cats jumping champions is their bone structure. Their hind limbs are equipped with powerful muscles and a long spinal column, which acts as a spring, storing energy for the jump.

Cats are also capable of controlling their body during the jump, thanks to their tail, which acts as a balancer and helps them maintain stability in mid-air. However, not all cats are able to jump as high. The ability to jump also depends on their size and weight. Lighter cats, such as Siamese cats, are generally able to jump higher compared to larger-sized cats.

Jumping is a fundamental skill for cats, both for capturing prey and escaping danger. Thanks to their incredible agility, cats have always been regarded as mysteriously fascinating creatures. But beyond myths and legends, the truth is that cats are truly extraordinary animals, endowed with incredible physical abilities and astonishing intuition.

Gorillas can learn sign language

Gorillas are extremely intelligent and social animals, capable of learning and communicating through a highly sophisticated language. One of the ways in which gorillas can communicate is through sign language, which involves a series of hand and body movements to convey meaning.

Gorillas have been the subject of intensive studies in the field of animal linguistics, particularly for their ability to learn sign language. For example, Koko was a famous gorilla trained to use American Sign Language, learning over a thousand words and demonstrating a highly advanced understanding of syntax and grammar within the language.

Furthermore, gorillas in the wild also use a range of vocal signals and body communication to interact with each other. These signals can convey various meanings, from danger alerts to territorial claims.

Gorillas are capable of learning from their companions, who help them acquire new skills and knowledge. This is particularly evident in captive gorilla communities, where the animals have greater opportunities to interact with humans and learn sign language.

Gorillas are highly intelligent and communicative animals, utilizing a wide range of signals and languages to communicate with each other and with humans. Their ability to learn sign language is an example of their extraordinary intelligence and their capacity to learn and adapt to different situations they encounter.

Frogs can absorb water through their skin

Frogs are animals that primarily live in aquatic or humid environments. But in addition to breathing through their lungs, frogs are capable of absorbing water through their skin. This ability is called cutaneous absorption.

The skin of frogs is rich in mucous glands that produce a substance called mucus, which helps keep the skin moist and protects against infections. But this ability of cutaneous absorption also allows frogs to absorb the water necessary for their survival.

Specifically, frogs absorb water through their skin during cutaneous respiration. This process occurs when frogs immerse their bodies in water and the skin absorbs dissolved oxygen, along with any other substances present in the water such as minerals and chemicals.

The ability to absorb water through the skin is crucial for the survival of frogs during periods of drought. When water is not readily available nearby, frogs can bury themselves in moist soil to avoid dehydration and use their skin to absorb the water necessary to survive.

The skin of frogs is highly permeable, which means they can absorb chemical substances and pollutants present in the water and the surrounding environment. This makes frogs particularly sensitive to environmental changes and threats to the ecosystem.

The ability of frogs to absorb water through their skin is a fundamental feature for their survival in aquatic or humid environments, as well as for their ability to adapt to unfavorable environmental conditions. However, this feature also makes frogs particularly vulnerable to pollutants and environmental threats, requiring special attention for their conservation and protection.

Flamingos can sleep while standing

Flamingos are known for their unusual sleeping posture: standing on one leg. However, this behavior is not due to their inability to sleep lying down, but rather a conscious choice of the birds to protect themselves from predators while sleeping.

The ability of flamingos to sleep while standing is made possible by the structure of their legs, which are long and thin, with a knee that bends upward instead of sideways like in the legs of other birds. This position allows them to rest most of their weight on one leg while the other rests.

Furthermore, flamingos have developed an automatic locking mechanism in the joints of their legs, which prevents them from falling while sleeping standing up. This mechanism works by relaxing the muscles in their legs, allowing the joints to automatically lock, so that the bird remains in an upright position effortlessly.

Although it may seem strange, sleeping while standing is a very practical choice for flamingos, as they are often exposed to predators such as alligators and crocodiles that inhabit the shallow waters where they feed. The upright position allows them to wake up quickly and escape in case of danger.

Sleeping while standing allows flamingos to cool their bodies by maintaining a small contact area between their feet and the ground. This process, known as thermoregulation, helps maintain the flamingos' body temperature constant, ensuring good health.

Mice can survive without water longer than camels

The mouse is a remarkable animal in many ways, but perhaps its most exceptional trait is its ability to survive without water for long periods of time. In fact, mice can survive without water for longer periods than camels, which are known for their ability to withstand long periods of drought.

Mice can keep their bodies hydrated through the food they eat. Most foods contain some amount of water, and mice can extract this water and use it to keep their bodies hydrated. Additionally, mice can concentrate their urine to conserve water in their bodies.

Mice also can regulate their body temperature efficiently, which reduces the amount of water lost through perspiration. Furthermore, mice can minimize water loss through respiration.

In nature, mice inhabit many different environments, including arid and desert regions where water is scarce. Their ability to survive without water helps them thrive in these challenging environments.

Mice are highly adaptable animals that have developed mechanisms to survive in harsh, water-deprived environments. Their ability to survive without water for long periods of time is a remarkable trait and showcases just how resilient these small creatures truly are.

Dogs can sniff out cancer

Dogs have an incredibly powerful sense of smell, and it has long been known that these animals can detect many things that humans cannot perceive. In recent years, there have been many studies that have shown that dogs can also sniff out cancer.

When a person has cancer, their body produces volatile compounds that dogs can detect. Additionally, when a person is sick, their body odor changes, making it easier for dogs to detect diseases.

There have been many studies demonstrating that dogs can sniff out cancer. In a 2011 study, dogs were trained to detect lung cancer through scent. In another 2013 study, dogs were trained to detect breast cancer.

In a 2019 study, researchers trained dogs to detect blood cancer. This study showed that dogs achieved an accuracy rate of 97% in detecting blood cancer.

Training dogs to detect cancer can be very useful in early diagnosis of the disease. This is particularly important for tumors that often go undiagnosed until it is too late.

Dogs can be used to detect cancer in a non-invasive way, avoiding the need for painful blood tests or biopsies. There are already several ongoing studies testing the effectiveness of dogs in early cancer detection in various types of tumors.

Dogs can sniff out cancer with remarkable accuracy. This ability can be used to improve early cancer diagnosis and help people receive necessary treatment as soon as possible.

Giant pandas eat almost exclusively bamboo

The giant panda, also known as the "panda bear," is a unique and recognizable animal belonging to the bear family. While most bears are carnivorous, the giant panda is primarily herbivorous, with 99% of its diet consisting of bamboo.

These animals live atop mountains in the central regions of China, where temperatures are cold and bamboo forests are abundant. They are typically solitary, except during the mating season and cub-rearing.

What makes the giant panda so special is its evolutionary adaptation to eating bamboo. Despite belonging to the bear family, its digestive system is more akin to that of carnivores, making it unable to efficiently digest bamboo cellulose. As a result, the giant panda must consume enormous quantities of bamboo to meet its caloric needs.

Their digestive tract has been adapted to process large amounts of bamboo, which is highly fibrous and difficult to digest. Their teeth are large and flat, helping them crush the tough bamboo stems. Additionally, their intestine is long and complex, allowing the bamboo to remain in the intestine for an extended period, enabling bacteria to break it down more efficiently.

Despite their affinity for bamboo, giant pandas are not entirely devoid of animal proteins. They also feed on insects, rodents, and occasionally encounter the carcasses of deceased animals.

Unfortunately, the giant panda is an endangered species due to habitat destruction and illegal hunting. However, thanks to conservation efforts, their population is slowly increasing, and we hope they can continue to thrive in their bamboo forests for many years to come.

Lions can reach a speed of 80 miles per hour

Lions, animals known for their powerful presence and majesty, can reach impressive speeds. Although they are not the fastest felines, lions can still achieve an impressive speed of around 50 miles per hour.

The speed of lions is particularly useful when they hunt their prey. They use their strength and speed to chase the prey, corner it, and then attack. Additionally, lions use their speed to defend their territory and their family.

However, not all lions are equally fast. The maximum speed can vary depending on the size, sex, and physical condition of the animal. Male lions tend to be larger and stronger than females, but females are usually more agile and fast.

In general, lions are highly adaptable animals that know how to use their strength and speed to survive in a variety of different environments. Their ability to run fast is just one of the many attributes that make them so unique and fascinating.

Owls can rotate their necks up to 270 degrees

Owls are nocturnal birds that have perfectly adapted to the nighttime environment. Their ability to fly silently, locate prey in the darkness, and move with agility among trees has fascinated humans for centuries. But there is another characteristic that sets them apart from other birds: their ability to rotate their necks by 270 degrees.

Contrary to what one might think, the ability of owls to rotate their necks is not due to the number of vertebrae they have, which is like that of other birds. Instead, owls have an incredibly flexible neck, which can rotate thanks to the joints located at the base of the skull.

The reason why owls can rotate their necks so impressively is because they have very limited binocular vision, meaning they cannot see with both eyes simultaneously. Therefore, to compensate for this limitation, owls need to be able to rotate their necks to have a panoramic view of the surrounding environment.

However, despite their ability to rotate their necks, owls cannot rotate their heads by 360 degrees, as one might think. Additionally, rotating the neck too quickly can be harmful to them, as it can lead to problems with blood circulation.

The ability of owls to rotate their necks by 270
degrees is an astonishing adaptation for their
limited binocular vision, allowing them to have
a panoramic view of the surrounding nighttime
environment. However, it is important to remember that this ability does not mean that owls
can rotate their heads by 360 degrees or do so
without negative consequences for their health.

Snakes do not have external ears, but they can sense vibrations through their skin

Snakes are animals that have fascinated humanity for centuries, thanks to their ability to move quickly and agilely, and for their somewhat mysterious and often dangerous appearance. But one thing that many people don't know about snakes is that, despite not having external ears, they are able to sense vibrations through their skin.

Snakes have a series of sensory organs called "Jacobson's organs," which are located on the upper part of their palate. These organs function like an "internal nose" that allows snakes to detect odor molecules in the air. But these organs are not only used for the sense of smell: they are also capable of sensing ground vibrations.

When a snake moves, it creates vibrations through the ground with its body. These vibrations propagate through the terrain and are detected by the Jacobson's organs. This sensory system is particularly useful for snakes that live in dark environments where vision is not well developed. For example, snakes that live underground, like the blind snake, rely heavily on vibrations to locate prey.

Another interesting fact is that snakes cannot hear sounds like humans do. This is because they lack external ears and only have an opening on the cranial bone. However, some snakes, like the king cobra, can sense sound waves through the movement of their cranial bones.

In general, snakes are highly skilled and adaptable animals, capable of surviving in many different situations. Their ability to sense vibrations through their skin is just one of the many fascinating traits that make these animals so unique.

Crabs can regenerate their claws

Crabs are animals that live in saltwater or freshwater. They are known for their unique characteristics, including the ability to regenerate their lost limbs. This ability has been extensively studied by scientists, but the exact mechanism is still not fully understood.

The regeneration of limbs in crabs occurs through a process called epimorphic regeneration. When a limb is lost, the crab develops a bulge on the body where the limb was attached. This bulge contains undifferentiated cells, called blastemal cells, which can differentiate into any type of tissue needed for the new limb.

The blastemal cells begin to proliferate and differentiate, creating new tissue for the limb. Eventually, the new tissue transforms into a fully functional limb. The speed at which this process occurs depends on the crab species and the environmental conditions it is in.

In addition to limb regeneration, crabs are known for many other interesting features. For example, many crabs have one larger claw than the other, which they use for defense or capturing food. Some crabs can also change color to blend in with their surroundings.

Crabs are fascinating animals and have been extensively studied by scientists for many years. Their ability to regenerate limbs is just one of the many intriguing aspects of their biology.

Dogs can only sweat through their paws

Dogs are beloved pets all around the world. They are often considered among man's best friends for their loyalty and devotion. However, there are many interesting facts about these animals that we often overlook.

One intriguing fact about dogs pertains to their sweating system. Unlike humans, who sweat through their skin, dogs do not have sweat glands all over their bodies. Instead, they have sweat glands only in their paws. This means that dogs can only sweat through their paws.

Why don't dogs sweat like humans? The answer lies in evolution. Throughout evolution, dogs have developed this sweating system because they live in very different environments compared to humans. In nature, dogs are highly active animals and spend a lot of time running and playing. Sweating through their paws helps cool their bodies when they are active.

Furthermore, dogs have other techniques for cooling themselves. For instance, they can pant rapidly through their mouths, increasing air circulation and cooling their bodies. They may also seek out a cool shade or a place with water to refresh themselves.

Dogs are wonderful creatures with unique characteristics that make them very special. Their
sweating system through their paws is just one
of the many intriguing facts about their lives that
make them so interesting and fascinating.

Pelicans use their enormous beak pouches to collect food

Pelicans are known for their characteristic beak pouch, a wide and deep sac that extends from the lower jaw and can hold up to 13 liters of water. But did you know that these birds also use their pouches to capture and collect food?

Pelicans are efficient predators that primarily feed on fish. When they spot a fish, they quickly dive into the water and snatch it with their long, pointed beak. However, if the fish is too large to be swallowed immediately, the pelican holds it in its beak pouch, where the water drains out through the holes at the bottom, leaving only the fish.

This beak pouch also proves useful for gathering food in times of scarcity. Pelicans can store food in their beak pouch and bring it back to the colony to feed their young or save it for a later meal. Additionally, the beak pouch can also be used for cooling down in excessive heat.

The beak pouch of pelicans is not just a strange and curious appendage, but it also plays an important role in their feeding and survival.

Owls can see in total darkness

Owls are known for their ability to see in total darkness. They are among the most famous nocturnal birds and have special adaptations that allow them to hunt and fly at night. One of their most remarkable adaptations is their ability to see in low-light conditions.

Their eyes are very large compared to their head, and they can gather lighter than the eyes of other birds. Additionally, they have many light-sensitive cells, known as rods, in their retinas, which allow them to see in low-light conditions.

Owls' eyes are also capable of quickly adapting to changes in light, which means they can transition rapidly from darkness to bright light without compromising their vision.

But vision is not the only sense owls use to navigate in the dark. They are also able to locate prey through sound. Owls have highly developed hearing and use their hearing to locate prey and navigate in darkness.

Their left ear is slightly lower than the right ear, which allows them to distinguish the vertical position of sound sources, helping them better locate their prey.

Owls are among the most adaptable nocturnal animals and have a unique combination of vision and hearing that makes them skilled night hunters. Their ability to see in total darkness has made them a symbol of wisdom and mystery and has made them the protagonists of many stories and legends.

Parrots can learn to imitate human speech

Parrots are known for their ability to speak and imitate sounds. But how do they learn to reproduce human words and phrases? The answer lies in their capacity for imitation and learning.

Parrots have a brain area called the "parrot nucleus," which is believed to be involved in the processing and production of language. They can reproduce sounds and words they have heard repeatedly, and with proper training, they can also learn to pronounce specific words.

To train a parrot to speak, it's important to start with short and simple phrases and repeat them often. Over time, the parrot will learn to repeat the words and, if encouraged, pronounce them more accurately.

However, not all parrots are capable of learning to speak. The ability to imitate largely depends on the species of parrot and its individual personality. Some are more inclined to learn human language than others.

Parrots can become highly entertaining and interactive companions. Their ability to reproduce human words and sounds makes them unique and beloved by many pet owners.

Lemurs have a highly developed sense of smell that helps them find food

Lemurs are nocturnal animals that live exclusively on the island of Madagascar. These primates have a unique sense of smell that allows them to find food even in low-light conditions.

The sense of smell in lemurs is developed through the presence of an organ called the "olfactory bulb," which is particularly large and complex compared to other primates. Additionally, lemurs can detect chemical substances in the air through a structure called the "rhinarium," located in their nasal cavity.

This olfactory ability is particularly useful for lemurs, as many of the plants they feed on emit chemical substances that can only be detected through smell. Moreover, smell is also important for communication among individuals within the same group, as lemurs use chemical substances to mark their territory and signal their reproductive status.

In general, smell is a crucial sense for nocturnal animals, as vision and hearing can be limited in low-light conditions. Lemurs are just one example of nocturnal animals that have developed a highly developed sense of smell to survive in such conditions.

Camels can survive for months without water

Camels are known for their ability to survive in extreme environments and under water scarcity conditions. In fact, they can go without drinking water for a period that can extend up to months. This is because camels can conserve water in their bodies through various adaptive strategies.

Firstly, their diet primarily consists of dry plants that contain very little water but are rich in nutrients. This allows camels to absorb sufficient water from the food they eat.

Additionally, camels have highly efficient kidneys that filter water in a concentrated manner, producing highly concentrated and dry urine. This way, camels lose very little water through urine.

Camels also can minimize water loss through respiration, thanks to certain unique features of their nose and mouth.

However, it is important to note that camels cannot live without water indefinitely, and although they are highly adaptable, they need to drink regularly to maintain their health and well-being.

Swans can remember the people who have helped them in the past

Swans are known for their grace and beauty, but what may not be widely known is that these elegant birds are also highly intelligent and have exceptional memory. Swans can remember people who have helped them in the past and can show a preference for those who have treated them kindly.

In a study conducted at the University of Bristol in the United Kingdom, researchers demonstrated that swans can remember individuals up to three years after encountering them and can differentiate between those who have assisted them and those who have not.

The research team conducted the experiment by visiting a pond where several swans resided. They approached the birds and fed them bread, but only certain swans accepted the food. Later, the researchers attempted to approach the same swans without any food, but the birds displayed signs of nervousness and kept their distance.

After three years, the researchers returned to the same pond and attempted to approach the swans again. The swans that had previously accepted the food approached the researchers, while those that had not received any food moved away.

This study demonstrates that swans have exceptional memory and can distinguish between individuals who have helped them and those who have not. This ability to remember can also aid swans in avoiding predators and recalling migratory routes.

Swans are also known for their protective behavior towards their young. They can become highly aggressive if they sense their offspring are threatened and may even attack humans if they feel threatened.

Swans are marvelous creatures with exceptional memory and a strong ability to protect their young. These elegant birds continue to astonish us with their intelligence and captivating behavior.

Wolves can howl to communicate with other members of their pack several kilometers away

Wolves are social animals that live in organized packs. One of their most recognizable features is howling, a powerful and penetrating sound they can emit to communicate with other members of the pack. The howl of the wolf has an incredible range and can be heard for kilometers.

The howling of wolves serves several purposes within the pack. Firstly, it helps maintain the social cohesion of the group. When one wolf howls, other pack members respond with their own howls, creating a unique chorus that helps establish the location and presence of everyone. This form of communication helps strengthen bonds between pack members and maintains a sense of unity.

Additionally, wolf howling also serves to signal the presence of the pack and mark territory. Howls can be heard over significant distances and serve as a warning to other wolves or potential intruders. In this way, wolves communicate their presence and assert the territory they consider theirs.

Wolf howling is also associated with communication during hunting. During pack hunting, wolves use howls and other sounds to coordinate their actions and strategies. This form of communication enables them to hunt more effectively and maximize their chances of success.

Wolf howling can be considered a form of emotional expression. Wolves can howl to express joy, frustration, fear, or pain. These different types of howls can convey information about an individual's emotional state to other pack members and contribute to maintaining social balance within the group.

The howling of wolves is a complex form of communication that allows them to maintain social cohesion, mark territory, coordinate hunting, and express emotions. This vocal communication is essential for the survival and success of a wolf pack.

Octopuses are highly intelligent creatures and can solve complex problems

Octopuses are highly intelligent and curious marine creatures. Despite their unusual appearance, they possess a highly developed brain with a great capacity for learning and memory.

One of the most astonishing aspects of their intelligence is their ability to solve complex problems. In a 2009 study, an octopus was placed in an aquarium with a jar of food sealed with a lid. After unsuccessfully attempting to open the lid, the octopus noticed a valve on the top of the jar that released water. The octopus learned to manipulate the valve to drain the water from the jar, causing the lid to fall off and providing access to the food.

In addition to problem-solving abilities, octopuses are skilled learners and possess the capacity for memory. In another study, an octopus was trained to identify different symbols to receive food. After being exposed to the symbols for only a few days, the octopus successfully learned to identify them and demonstrated long-term memory capabilities.

Octopuses are also known for their ability to camouflage and hide from predators. They can rapidly change the color and texture of their skin to blend in with their surroundings and elude the sight of potential threats.

Furthermore, octopuses can use tools to accomplish their goals. In a 2011 study, an octopus was observed utilizing a coconut shell as protection and hiding place. The octopus selected a shell, cleaned it, rolled it to its shelter, and used it as a door.

Octopuses are extremely intelligent and curious marine creatures, capable of solving complex problems, learning, memorizing, camouflaging, and using tools. Their intelligence is astounding and continues to astonish scientists as they strive to comprehend the intricacies of their world.

Clownfish live in symbiosis with sea anemones

Clownfish, also known as "Nemo," thanks to the famous character from the animated film of the same name, are among the most well-known and iconic tropical fish species. These fish live in symbiosis with sea anemones, benefiting mutually.

Sea anemones are marine animals that have long tentacles containing stinging cells called nematocysts, which they use to defend against predators and capture food. Clownfish, on the other hand, have a thin mucous coating that protects them from the stinging nematocysts and renders them immune to the anemone's venom.

Clownfish live inside the anemones, taking refuge among their tentacles to protect themselves from predators and performing a dance to stimulate the anemone to produce more nematocysts, which in turn deter predators. In return, clownfish produce nutrient-rich feces that anemones can utilize for their growth and reproduction.

This symbiotic relationship between clownfish and sea anemones is an example of how animals can coexist and benefit from each other. Furthermore, this symbiosis is an important source of sustenance for many coastal communities around the world, as clownfish are a highly valued fish species in culinary contexts.

Rabbits can jump up to three times their own length

Rabbits are known for their ability to jump agilely and with great precision. Despite their relatively small size, rabbits are capable of impressive leaps, reaching up to three times their own length.

The physical structure of rabbits contributes to their jumping ability. Their hind legs are particularly strong and muscular, with elastic joints that act like powerful springs. This allows them to store and release energy rapidly during the jump. Additionally, rabbits have padded feet that act as propellers, enabling them to push forcefully against the ground and achieve greater propulsion.

Rabbits use their jumps for various purposes. One of the main reasons is to escape from predators. With their agility and speed, rabbits can quickly evade danger by leaping away. Furthermore, jumps allow them to reach higher areas to evade potential threats.

But rabbits don't just jump to escape. During courtship, males may perform acrobatic jumps to attract the attention of females. These jumps demonstrate their strength and vitality, signaling their suitability as reproductive partners.

It is fascinating to observe rabbits as they show-case their agile and dynamic jumps. These captivating creatures demonstrate remarkable skill in overcoming obstacles and moving gracefully in their natural environment. Their spectacular leaps are a clear example of the wonders and extraordinary abilities of animals in the animal kingdom.

Falcons can fly at speeds exceeding 200 miles per hour

The falcon is one of the fastest predators in the animal kingdom. Thanks to its aerodynamic shape and the muscular power of its wings, it can fly at speeds exceeding 200 miles per hour. This makes it one of the most skilled raptors in hunting its prey, which can be other birds, rodents, and insects.

The falcon can reach such speeds thanks to its anatomy, which allows it to glide over long distances and move rapidly in a dive. Additionally, its vision is very keen, allowing it to spot prey even at great distances.

But it's not just the speed that makes the falcon such a skilled predator: its sharp beak and powerful talons enable it to grasp and kill prey precisely and swiftly. Moreover, the falcon can adapt to a wide range of habitats, from the desert to the rainforest, which allows it to survive in many parts of the world.

Despite its menacing appearance, the falcon is a very fascinating and respected animal. Its flying abilities have been extensively studied by scientists, and its allure has made it a popular figure in popular culture.

Foxes have a highly developed sense of hearing that aids them in hunting their prey

Foxes are highly skilled and intelligent animals that have been the subject of many legends and folktales. But in addition to their thieving and cunning abilities, these animals have a highly developed sense of hearing that aids them in hunting.

Foxes have large and mobile ears that can rotate up to 180 degrees, allowing the animal to pinpoint the source of a sound with great precision. Furthermore, foxes can distinguish between different types of sounds, such as bird songs or frog croaks, and they can use this knowledge to locate their prey.

Foxes can locate prey through sound even if it is hidden under the snow or underground. Additionally, when foxes hunt in pairs, they use their hearing ability to communicate with each other and coordinate their hunting.

Foxes are also capable of hearing sounds from long distances. For example, they can perceive sounds produced by other animals several kilometers away. This ability is particularly important for male foxes, as they need to locate females in heat and defend their territory from intruders.

The developed hearing of foxes is an important skill that enables them to hunt successfully and communicate with other members of their pack. Without this ability, the survival of foxes would be much more challenging.

Sloths spend most of their lives hanging from tree branches

Sloths are curious and interesting animals. They spend most of their lives hanging from tree branches thanks to their long and powerful claws, which they use to grip and support their bodies for long periods of time.

These animals are known for their slowness and for spending much of their lives sleeping or resting. They are solitary creatures but can occasionally share the same tree with other sloths.

Sloths are also known for their leaf-based diet. They can only digest a small number of leaves at a time and take a long time to move from one tree to another in search of food.

Despite their slowness, sloths have developed some unique features to defend themselves against predators. For example, their fur grows in the opposite direction compared to other mammals, which helps them blend in when clinging to trees.

Sloths can emit high-frequency sounds to deter predators such as snakes and birds of prey. These sounds are imperceptible to the human ear but can be heard by other animals.

Sloths are fascinating animals that spend most of their lives hanging from trees, sleeping, resting, and feeding on leaves. Despite their slowness, these animals have developed unique characteristics to survive in their natural environment, defending themselves against predators and remaining hidden.

Zebras can emit a sound like a "sucking" noise to communicate with their herd

Zebras are social animals that live in large herds and communicate with each other in various ways. One of the most interesting modes of communication is the emission of a distinct sound, resembling a suction noise, which is used to alert other members of the herd to a potential danger or imminent threat.

This sound is very useful as it allows zebras to communicate over long distances, even in the presence of background noise or other factors that may interfere with verbal communication. Additionally, each zebra has a distinctive sound that enables them to recognize one another and identify members of their own herd.

Zebras also use other signals to communicate with each other, such as body language and the emission of different sounds. For example, a zebra may emit a sound like a neigh to call its foal or to get the attention of another herd member.

Zebras also communicate through their movement patterns. When they are frightened or agitated, zebras tend to move erratically, running in circles or jumping. On the contrary, when they are relaxed and secure, they walk calmly and steadily.

Zebras are highly social and communicative animals that use various signals to interact with each other and ensure the survival of the herd. Their distinct suction-like sound is one of the most intriguing aspects of their behavior and represents an important form of communication in their world.

Red pandas are the only mammals that can absorb uric acid, reducing the amount of urine they need to produce

Red pandas are adorable creatures that inhabit the mountainous forests of the Himalayas and surrounding regions. One of the remarkable characteristics of these animals is their ability to efficiently absorb uric acid, a waste substance produced by their metabolism.

Unlike other mammals, red pandas have an adapted system that allows them to convert uric acid into other less harmful substances for their bodies. This process, known as allantoinuria, enables them to reduce the amount of urine they need to produce and conserve water within their organism.

This adaptation is particularly important for red pandas as they live in mountain habitats where water is often limited. Thanks to their ability to absorb uric acid, these animals can survive even with a low amount of available water.

The red pandas' ability to manage uric acid so efficiently is a distinctive trait of this species. It is interesting to note that this characteristic is not shared with other animals, making red pandas unique in their kind.

Water conservation through the absorption of uric acid is just one of the many adaptations that allow red pandas to survive in the harsh mountain environment. These animals primarily feed on bamboo leaves, which provide them with the energy needed to sustain their metabolism and keep them active.

Red pandas are fascinating creatures that have developed a unique mechanism to manage uric acid in their bodies. This adaptation is essential for their survival in the mountainous regions they inhabit, allowing them to reduce the amount of urine produced and conserve precious water resources.

Rabbits can produce up to 200 droppings per day

The rabbit is an animal known for its ability to produce large quantities of droppings. In fact, an adult rabbit can produce up to 200 droppings per day. This is because their digestive system is designed to only partially digest the food they eat. In this way, they can extract the maximum nutritional value from the food and minimize waste.

The droppings of rabbits are different from normal animal feces as they are spherical, small, and very hard. This is because they contain a large amount of dietary fiber and other nutrients such as proteins and vitamins that the rabbit has extracted from the food during digestion.

Additionally, rabbits have another special intestinal feature called the cecum, which is responsible for the production of cecotropes. Cecotropes are a type of soft, sticky feces that the rabbit immediately ingests after producing them. This process is known as coprophagy and allows the rabbit to obtain a greater amount of nutrients from the food.

The large quantity of feces produced by rabbits is not due to a poor diet or an inefficient digestive system, but rather to a sophisticated mechanism to extract the maximum nutritional value from the food they eat.

Lizards can change their color to blend in with the surrounding environment

Lizards are famous for their ability to change color, a phenomenon known as "color change." This remarkable feature allows them to camouflage with the surrounding environment and adapt to different situations.

The color change in lizards is made possible by specialized cells in their skin called chromatophores. Chromatophores contain pigments, such as melanin, that can vary in quantity and distribution. When these pigments contract or expand, they influence the lizard's skin color.

The ability of lizards to change color depends on various factors, including mood, temperature, light, and the need for camouflage. For example, if a lizard is in an environment with a dark background, it may darken its skin to better blend in. Similarly, if it is excited or feels threatened, it may change color to communicate its emotional state to other individuals.

Not all lizards are capable of completely changing their color, but many species can significantly alter their appearance. Some lizards can transition from shades of green to brown, while others may display different colored bands or spots on their skin.

The color change in lizards is an exceptional
form of adaptation that offers them numerous
advantages. The ability to blend in with the surrounding environment allows them to evade
predators and approach prey unnoticed. Additionally, they can also use color change as a
means of social communication within their own
species.

The color change in lizards is a fascinating characteristic that reveals their ability to adapt to the
surrounding environment. This adaptation is essential for their survival and represents an example of the extraordinary diversity and complexity present in the animal world.

Beavers can fell large trees with their teeth

Beavers are known for their ability to build dams and lodges along watercourses. But what makes these creatures even more extraordinary is their incredible ability to fell large trees with their sharp teeth.

The teeth of beavers continuously grow throughout their lives, and for this reason, they need to keep gnawing on hard objects to prevent them from growing too much. This process not only keeps their teeth healthy but also enables them to bring down entire trees.

Beavers have powerful jaw muscles and a system of incisors and molars that work in synergy to cut trees. They use their front teeth to nibble away at the bark and inner layers of the tree, and once they have dug deep enough, they start pushing the tree until it falls.

This skill of beavers to fell trees is essential for their survival, as fallen trees are crucial for building dams and lodges. Once the trees are felled, beavers drag them into the water and use them to construct their hydraulic engineering works.

Furthermore, the falling of trees creates a cascade effect on the surrounding ecosystem, resulting in the formation of new habitats and the creation of open spaces where plants can grow and thrive.

The ability of beavers to fell trees is a testament to their physical strength and their ability to shape the surrounding environment. Without them, many species of animals and plants would not have suitable habitats to live and thrive.

Sea turtles can travel for hundreds of miles to lay their eggs

Sea turtles are incredible creatures that are capable of traveling hundreds of miles to lay their eggs. These turtles can migrate from their feeding areas to their nesting areas, which are often located far apart.

During the breeding season, female turtles leave their feeding grounds and swim to the beaches where they were born to lay their eggs. The journey is perilous, as turtles are often preyed upon or accidentally caught in fishing nets.

Once they finally reach the beach, turtles choose a suitable spot to dig a nest where they will deposit their eggs. After laying the eggs, turtles cover the nest with sand to conceal it from predators. They then return to the sea and resume their migration journey back to their feeding areas.

The migration journey of sea turtles is an incredible and fascinating natural event. However, sea turtle populations are threatened by marine pollution, coastal development, and global warming. Protecting these species is of utmost importance to preserve the biodiversity of oceans and coastal ecosystems.

Owls can move their eyes to look in different directions simultaneously

Owls are nocturnal animals, known for their ability to see in complete darkness thanks to their large eyes. But that's not all: these birds can also move their eyes to look in different directions simultaneously, without having to turn their heads. This means they can scan the surrounding environment without having to move their bodies and maintain maximum control over the situation.

This feature is possible due to the anatomical structure of owl eyes, which are tubular in shape and positioned forward in their heads. This allows them to perceive the movements of animals outside their direct line of sight and track their movements accurately.

Furthermore, owls have very sharp vision, enabling them to see small objects even in low-light conditions. Their ability to perceive shapes and details is so developed that they can spot prey even when it is completely camouflaged in the surrounding environment.

Owls are highly adaptable and intelligent animals, capable of successfully hunting even in challenging conditions. Thanks to their exceptional vision, they can spot prey at remarkable distances and capture it with great precision.

Ants are capable of lifting objects up to 50 times their body weight

Ants are small but incredibly strong creatures. They are capable of lifting objects that weigh up to 50 times their body weight. This is possible due to their body structure and the strength of their jaws. Ants work together in groups to carry objects much larger than themselves, communicating with each other through chemical signals called pheromones.

In addition to their physical strength, ants have a highly advanced social system. Each ant has a specific role within the colony, and ants work together to ensure the survival of the colony itself. There are worker ants, responsible for foraging for food and caring for the young, soldier ants that protect the colony from external threats, and a queen that lays eggs.

Ants are also capable of solving complex problems. For example, if a worker ant finds a food source, it will leave a trail of pheromones to indicate to other ants where the food is located. The ants will then follow the pheromone trail to reach the food source, creating a highly effective communication system.

Ants can create intricate structures within their colonies, such as chambers and tunnels, using soil and other materials they find in the surrounding environment. These structures are often highly elaborate and serve a specific purpose within the colony.

Ants are extraordinary creatures, possessing incredible strength, a complex social system, and the ability to solve complex problems. Although they are often considered a nuisance, ants play an important role in the ecosystem and in our understanding of animal behavior.

Dogs can perceive the emotional tone of the human voice

Dogs are known for their ability to understand and respond to human communication. These animals have been shown to be able to perceive the emotional tone of the human voice.

A study conducted in 2016 demonstrated that dogs can distinguish between words spoken with a happy tone and words spoken with an angry tone. Dogs can also perceive changes in vocal tone, such as when a person transitions from happiness to anger or vice versa.

In another study conducted in 2018, researchers found that dogs can use the intensity of the voice to determine a person's level of stress. When dogs were presented with a sample of human voices with different stress levels, they showed increased attention to the more stressed voices, demonstrating their ability to perceive and respond to human emotions.

Dogs have shown the ability to understand human body language, such as facial expressions and gestures. They can read human facial expressions and respond accordingly, demonstrating a remarkable sensitivity to their surroundings.

Dogs are animals endowed with remarkable emotional intelligence, allowing them to perceive and respond to human emotions. Their ability to perceive the emotional tone of the human voice makes them ideal companions for people seeking comfort and emotional support.

Bats have a system of echolocation that allows them to fly and hunt in the dark

Bats are nocturnal animals, but that doesn't prevent them from moving with agility and precision in the dark, without even colliding with obstacles. This is thanks to their echolocation system, a kind of natural "radar" that they use to navigate and find food.

The bat emits ultrasonic sounds through its mouth or nose, which travel through the air and bounce off objects and obstacles, creating an echo that is detected by the bat's ears. This system allows them to create a mental map of the surrounding environment and identify the presence of prey such as insects, spiders, or small vertebrates.

Furthermore, the bat's echolocation system is so precise that they can distinguish the shape, size, and speed of moving objects, even at several meters. This ability allows them to avoid obstacles during flight and capture moving prey.

Bats are highly skilled animals with a highly developed sensory system, which makes them particularly well-suited for nocturnal life and hunting in the dark. Their echolocation system has been studied for human applications, such as the development of navigation devices for the visually impaired or for monitoring moving objects.

Cheetahs can reach a top speed of 75 miles per hour in a matter of seconds

The cheetah is an animal that belongs to the felid family. This large feline, native to Africa and Asia, is known for its impressive speed, which allows it to reach a top speed of 75 miles per hour in a matter of seconds. The cheetah is the fastest land mammal in the world, enabling it to hunt its prey with great ease.

The cheetah has a slender and elongated body, with long and muscular legs that allow it to cover great distances with each stride. Its tail is long and flexible, serving as a rudder to maintain balance during the run. Its coat is a reddish-yellow color with distinct round black spots, and its eyes are large and brown.

The cheetah hunts both during the day and at night, but it prefers to hunt at dawn and dusk when temperatures are cooler. Its diet primarily consists of antelopes, gazelles, and other ungulates, but it can also hunt small mammals such as hares, rodents, and birds.

Despite its speed and agility, the cheetah is considered a vulnerable animal due to the loss of its natural habitat, hunting, and the reduction of prey availability. Wildlife conservation organizations work to protect the cheetah and its natural habitat, as well as to educate people on the importance of wildlife conservation.

Kangaroos have a pouch in which they carry their young

Kangaroos are native to Australia and are known for their ability to hop long distances with their powerful hind legs. But that's not their only distinctive feature: female kangaroos have a ventral pouch called a "marsupium" in which their young, called "joeys," can grow and develop safely.

The kangaroo's pouch is formed by a fold of skin that creates a sort of upward-facing bag where the joey can seek refuge from birth. Joeys are only a few centimeters long at birth and are blind and hairless, but they can climb into the mother's pouch and attaching to her nipple to feed on milk.

Once inside the pouch, the joey remains there for several weeks or months, depending on the species, until it is sufficiently large and developed to face the outside world. Initially, the young remain attached to the nipple for most of the time, but gradually starts venturing out of the pouch to explore the surrounding environment, always under the mother's protection.

The kangaroo's pouch is an example of a unique and extraordinary evolutionary adaptation that allows the young to develop safely and protected while the mother continues her daily activities. Moreover, the fact that the young kangaroo can directly nurse from the mother's milk without having to wait for her to stop or sit down makes it particularly suited for the mobile lifestyle that characterizes these animals.

Pumas are solitary and territorial animals.

The puma, also known as mountain lion or cougar, is a solitary and territorial animal found throughout much of the Americas. Pumas are large felines, known for their agility and ability to climb trees. They are carnivorous animals and primarily feed on deer, elk, and other forest animals.

Pumas are known to be highly territorial and will defend their territory against other pumas and other animals that may pose a threat. Adult males have territories that can span many square kilometers, while females tend to occupy smaller territories.

Although solitary, pumas occasionally encounter others of their species during the breeding season. During this period, males emit loud roars to attract females and compete for the opportunity to mate. Once the female has chosen a mate, the two animals may stay together for several days.

Pumas are nocturnal animals and have highly light-sensitive eyes. They are also very skilled hunters, using their agility and strength to bring down prey. They can run at speeds of over 60 km/h for short distances and can leap up to 5.5 meters in distance.

However, despite their power and hunting abilities, pumas are threatened by humans, habitat destruction, and illegal hunting. While their population remains relatively stable in some protected areas, in other parts of their range, their survival is at risk.

Dolphins can recognize themselves in the mirror

Self-recognition in the mirror is a rare ability in the animal kingdom, and one of the few animals that have demonstrated this capability are dolphins. These highly intelligent marine mammals have shown the ability to recognize themselves in the mirror during scientific experiments.

This type of behavior demonstrates that dolphins have a form of self-awareness, meaning they know that the reflection in the mirror represents their own image. This suggests that dolphins have a high level of self-awareness and awareness of their environment, and they may possess the capacity for self-consciousness.

Furthermore, dolphins have demonstrated many other advanced cognitive abilities, such as the ability to communicate with each other through a complex series of sounds, problem-solving skills, and long-term memory. All these characteristics make dolphins one of the most intelligent animals in the animal kingdom.

In addition to their intelligence, dolphins are also known for their ability to swim at high speeds and perform impressive acrobatics in the water. They are highly social animals that live in groups of varying sizes and have evolved to live and interact with their aquatic environment in a unique and specialized way.

Deer shed their antlers every year and regrow them again

The deer is one of the animals best known for its impressive antlers, which are mainly used in fights between males to access females during mating season. But did you know that deer shed their antlers every year and regrow them again?

In fact, the shedding of antlers in deer is a natural process that occurs every year in late winter or early spring. The process of antler shedding is called "moulting," and the new pair of antlers that grows is called "velvet."

The shedding of antlers is caused by a decrease in testosterone levels in the deer. This allows specialized cells at the base of the antlers, called "osteoclastic cells," to begin breaking down the bony part of the antlers, allowing the old antlers to fall off.

After the antlers shed, the growth of the new pair immediately begins. Initially, the growth is very fast, around 1 inch per day, but then it slows down. Antlers grow in a similar way to human hair and nails, as they are made of keratin, a protein also present in these tissues.

The shape and size of antlers can vary among different deer species, but in general, the larger the antlers, the higher the chances that the deer will attract the attention of females and defeat male rivals.

The shedding and regrowth of antlers in deer is a natural process that occurs every year. Not only does this allow deer to keep their antlers healthy and in shape, but it is also an important aspect of their life cycle and reproduction.

Butterflies can feel with their wings

Butterflies are fascinating and colorful creatures that inhabit our gardens and meadows. We know that butterflies use their wings to fly with grace and lightness, but did you know that they can also feel with their wings?

The wings of butterflies are much more than simple appendages used for flight. They are extremely sensitive and contain numerous sensory structures called "setae". These setae are equipped with small sensory hairs called "scallops" that can detect vibrations and sounds in the surrounding environment.

When butterflies fly, their wings constantly move, generating vibrations that are detected by the sensors on the wing setae. These sensors are very sensitive and can perceive vibrations caused by sound or other approaching insects.

Butterflies use this ability to perceive vibrations to orient themselves in space, to detect potential predators, or to locate mates during courtship. This sense of touch through the wings is crucial for the survival and reproduction of butterflies.

However, it is important to note that the perception system of butterflies through their wings is not as developed as that of other animals, such as bats with their echolocation system or dogs with their keen sense of smell. Butterflies are primarily visual and rely mainly on sight to orient themselves and communicate.

Butterflies can indeed perceive vibrations and sounds through their wings thanks to the sensors on the setae. This ability helps them survive in their environment and interact with the world around them, adding another element of wonder and complexity to these delicate and fascinating creatures.

Crocodiles can stay underwater for hours thanks to their ability to hold their breath

Crocodiles are among the most feared animals in the entire animal kingdom. These enormous reptiles are known for their strength, speed, and their ability to hunt with great skill. However, what many people don't know is that crocodiles also can hold their breath for long periods of time, allowing them to stay underwater for hours without needing to come up for air.

Crocodiles can hold their breath thanks to a system of stored oxygen in their blood. Essentially, their muscles contract to keep oxygen-rich blood in their lungs and circulatory system, enabling them to remain submerged underwater for extended periods.

This ability is particularly important for crocodiles, as they often prey on aquatic animals such as fish and turtles. Staying underwater for long periods means that crocodiles can act more effectively during hunting, taking advantage of the element of surprise to attack their prey.

However, not only can crocodiles hold their breath for extended periods of time, but their closest relatives, American alligators and Asian gharials, also possess this same ability. Other animals, such as whales and seals, are also known for their ability to hold their breath for long periods, but crocodiles remain among the absolute champions of this animal talent.

Chameleons can extend their tongue up to 1.5 times the length of their body to capture prey

Chameleons are known for their extraordinary abilities of camouflage and their fascinating appearance. But there is another surprising characteristic that distinguishes these reptiles: their incredible tongue. Chameleons are equipped with an extendable tongue that they can rapidly project to capture prey.

The tongue of chameleons is incredibly long and flexible. In some cases, it can be extended up to 1.5 times the length of their body. This means that a medium-sized chameleon, for example, could launch its tongue to reach a distant object up to one and a half meters away. It is truly an impressive feature!

The way chameleons use their tongue to capture prey is equally extraordinary. When they spot an insect or other small animal they want to catch, chameleons rapidly contract the muscles of their tongue. This action creates a sort of "spring-like" effect, causing the tongue to elongate and extend towards the prey with great speed.

Once the chameleon's tongue has reached its maximum extension, it attaches to the prey thanks to a small amount of sticky mucus on the tip. The prey is then quickly pulled back into the chameleon's mouth, where it can be swallowed.

This linguistic ability of chameleons is an extraordinary evolutionary adaptation that allows them to hunt with great precision and success. Their quick and extendable tongue is a formidable weapon in their hunting and a truly fascinating spectacle to behold.

Coral snakes have the most toxic venom in the world

Coral snakes are among the most lethal creatures in the animal kingdom due to their highly toxic venom. These snakes are known for their bright coloration with red, black, and yellow stripes that make them easily recognizable. Their venom consists of a potent neurotoxin that can quickly paralyze prey or cause death in humans within minutes.

The coral snake can inject enough venom to kill several humans with a single bite, although such attacks are very rare. Furthermore, unlike many other venomous snakes, the coral snake has relatively small fangs, making it more difficult to detect and handle.

However, not all coral snakes are equally venomous. There are several species of coral snakes worldwide, and their venom varies significantly in terms of toxicity. Additionally, not all coral snakes are aggressive towards humans and tend to attack only when threatened or provoked.

In any case, if one encounters a coral snake, the best course of action would be to keep a safe distance and seek the help of an expert or professional. With a little caution and respect, humans can coexist with these deadly serpents.

______

Sealions can sleep underwater, using one lung at a time

Seals are fascinating animals and highly skilled in the aquatic environment. Among their abilities is the ability to sleep underwater, using one lung at a time. This capability is crucial for their survival in open waters, where predators can attack from any direction.

To sleep underwater, seals relax and slow down their heart rate, reducing blood flow to the extremities of their bodies to keep warm blood in their vital organs. This allows them to remain still for long periods without needing to surface for a breath.

Seals also rely on their nervous system to stay alert during sleep. Through this mechanism, the brain continuously sends signals to the muscles to maintain position and balance underwater, preventing them from sinking.

However, sleeping underwater can be risky if seals fail to take a breath in time. For this reason, these animals must have good control over their breathing and constantly monitor their environment to avoid being caught off guard by a predator.

Toucans have a massive beak that appears disproportionate to the rest of their body, but it is very lightweight

Toucans are tropical birds found primarily in South America, but also in some parts of Africa and Asia. They are known for their distinctive enormous beak that appears disproportionate to the rest of their body. This beak is not only large but also very lightweight.

The toucan's beak is composed of an interesting combination of hollow bones and keratin. This makes it lighter and more manageable, allowing the bird to fly without being burdened by its beak. Despite its imposing appearance, the toucan's beak is also highly functional: it is used to reach for food, as a means of defense against predators, and to attract mates during reproduction.

Additionally, the toucan's beak plays an important role in regulating the bird's body temperature. In fact, the beak is highly vascularized and helps dissipate body heat. During hot days, toucans can use their beak as a radiator to cool down.

In nature, there are approximately 40 species of toucans, each with slightly different beak shapes and lengths. There are toucans with short and wide beaks, such as the Toco Toucan, and others with longer and narrower beaks, such as the Swainson's Toucan. However, all toucan species share the same distinctive appearance and the lightweight yet functional beak.

Bees can see ultraviolet rays and use them to find the nectar of flowers

Bees are insects known for their crucial role in plant pollination, but they also have exceptional vision. An interesting characteristic of bees is their ability to see ultraviolet rays, which are invisible to the human eye. This special visual ability allows them to effectively locate and exploit sources of flower nectar.

Flowers often use invisible visual signals to attract pollinators like bees. The petals of flowers reflect ultraviolet light differently than the rest of the visible spectrum. This creates a pattern that is invisible to human eyes but highly visible to bee eyes.

Bees, with their ability to see ultraviolet rays, can perceive these patterns and easily distinguish flowers that contain nectar. This advanced visual sense enables them to find food sources more easily and optimize nectar collection during their pollination activity.

Furthermore, bees can also use ultraviolet rays to navigate in space. They can utilize patterns of ultraviolet light from the sky to determine the direction and distance of their movements. This ability is particularly useful when bees are far away from their hive and need to find their way back.

Thanks to their ultraviolet vision, bees can perceive the world around them differently than humans. This ability helps them adapt to their environment and fulfill their important role in plant pollination.

Rhinoceroses have very poor eyesight but a highly developed sense of smell, which helps them find food

Rhinoceroses are unique and interesting animals. These mammals have very poor eyesight, but their sense of smell is highly developed and helps them find food. Rhinoceroses are herbivores and primarily feed on leaves, branches, shoots, and fruits of trees and shrubs. Their diet varies depending on the species and their habitat.

Rhinoceroses have very poor eyesight because they have a low number of photoreceptor cells in their retinas. This means they can only see things at a very close distance. However, their sense of smell is highly developed and can detect the scent of a predator from a kilometer away. They can also distinguish the smells of their own kind, both males and females, which helps them in reproduction.

Rhinoceroses also use their sense of smell to find food, which is often hidden among tree branches and leaves. With their large noses, they can sniff the air to locate the plants they feed on.

Unfortunately, rhinoceroses are currently at risk of extinction due to poaching for their horns. In some cultures, rhino horn is considered a symbol of status and is used in traditional medicine. This illegal hunting is leading to a decrease in rhinoceros' populations worldwide, and efforts are needed to protect and preserve their species.

Caterpillars can eat up to 27,000 times their body weight before transforming into butterflies

Caterpillars are known to be voracious eaters and can consume incredible amounts of food before transforming into butterflies. In fact, they can eat up to 27,000 times their body weight during their larval life. This means that a 4-ounces caterpillar could consume 7 pounds of leaves before turning into a butterfly.

During their larval stage, caterpillars have an insatiable appetite as they need to accumulate enough energy and nutrients to support their metamorphosis. This process requires a lot of energy, as caterpillars have to completely dissolve their tissues and rebuild them into a completely different form.

However, not all caterpillars eat the same amount of food. Some caterpillars feed exclusively on leaves of a particular plant, while others are more generalists and can eat a wide range of plants. Additionally, the amount of food a caterpillar eats also depends on the species of the caterpillar, its age, and environmental conditions.

Their exceptional appetite is essential for their transformation into butterflies. After consuming enough leaves and accumulating sufficient energy, caterpillars attach themselves to a branch or leaf and transform into pupae. From this point onward, their bodies undergo an incredible process of transformation until they emerge as fully developed butterflies, ready to take flight.

The lemminis (small lemurs) are the smallest primates in the world

The lemminis, also known as pygmy lemurs, are the smallest primates in the world. These animals are endemic to Madagascar and can reach a length of only 4-6 inches and a weight of 1-1.5 ounces. Lemminis have a soft and dense reddish-brown fur, large dark eyes, and a long, slender tail that aids in balance during jumps between trees.

These animals are nocturnal and spend most of their time in the rainforests of Madagascar. They are social animals and live in groups that can range from two to twelve individuals. During the night, they move quickly among the trees in search of food, primarily insects and fruit.

Lemminis are highly agile animals and leap from one branch to another with great dexterity. They also have a highly developed sense of smell that helps them find food and identify other members of their group. Despite their small size, lemminis are very active animals and need to consume 25% of their body weight every night to survive.

Unfortunately, the population of lemminis is threatened by the destruction of their natural habitat due to deforestation. They are also victims of illegal hunting for the pet trade. The impact of human activities has caused a decline in their population, and their conservation status is considered vulnerable.

Cats can jump up to seven times their height

Cats are animals known for their agility and dexterity, and this is also reflected in their jumping ability. In fact, these domestic felines can jump up to 7 times their height, which means that a cat measuring 30 centimeters tall can jump up to 2.1 meters high. This is possible thanks to their bone and muscular structure, which is particularly suited for flexing and propelling their hind legs.

Furthermore, cats can adjust their position in mid-air to land precisely on their feet, without sustaining any harm or dangerous falls. This ability is made possible by the presence of an organ located in their inner ear, called the "vestibular apparatus," which allows them to maintain balance and orient themselves during jumps.

Not only can cats jump in height, but they can also leap in length and move agilely on narrow or elevated surfaces. However, it is important to remember that each cat has its own jumping ability, based on its size and physical condition. Additionally, jumping onto dangerous or high surfaces can be risky for the cat; therefore, it is important to pay attention to their safety and well-being.

Badgers build elaborate dens that can have up to 30 different entrances

Badgers are nocturnal animals that spend a large part of their time underground in their dens. These digging animals are known for their elaborate dens, which can have up to 30 different entrances and can extend for many meters below the ground.

Badger dens are typically made up of several different chambers, including feeding chambers, resting chambers, and even separate latrines. These animals also have a main entrance that is usually located in an open area, such as a meadow or field. Their dens can be large enough to accommodate up to 12 badgers at the same time.

One of the distinctive features of a badger den is its uppercase "A" shape, with a main corridor leading to the main chamber and side corridors branching off from the main corridor. This complex design provides protection and shelter not only for badgers but also for other animals, such as foxes, that may occupy abandoned badger dens.

Furthermore, badgers are known to be very clean and hygienic. They keep their dens and latrines separate, so as not to contaminate their resting and feeding areas with waste.

In general, badgers are highly territorial animals and can defend their dens fiercely when threatened. However, if left undisturbed, these animals are very shy and tend to avoid contact with humans. Their dens, on the other hand, can be found throughout Europe, Asia, and North America, where these animals continue to thrive in their intricate underground homes.

Kangaroos can jump up to three times their own height

Kangaroos are known for their jumping ability. In fact, they can jump up to three times their own height, which can reach up to 6 feet. This means that an adult kangaroo can jump up to 20 feet in length and 6 meters in height. Their strength and jumping ability are linked to their unique musculoskeletal system, which allows them to conserve energy when they jump.

Kangaroos also use their tail as a third foot, as it helps to balance their body during the jump. Their tail is long and muscular and can be used as a counterbalance for their body during the jump. Additionally, the kangaroo's tail also has an important communication function. When the kangaroo is in danger, it can thump its tail to alert other members of the group.

The kangaroo's jump is so powerful that it can even be dangerous for humans. There have been cases where kangaroos have jumped over moving cars, causing traffic accidents. However, kangaroos tend to be shy and non-aggressive creatures unless they feel threatened.

Kangaroos are incredibly adaptable and unique animals with impressive jumping abilities. They can jump up to three times their own height thanks to their musculoskeletal system and muscular tail.

Crocodiles can move their eyelids independently of each other

Crocodiles are fascinating and powerful animals, and one of their most interesting features is their ability to move their eyelids independently of each other. This means they can keep one eye open and the other closed simultaneously, which is very useful for hunting.

Crocodiles are opportunistic predators, which means they feed on anything they can catch, such as fish, reptiles, birds, mammals, and even other crocodiles. They are known for their immense strength and powerful jaws, which can easily crush the bones of their prey.

But their ability to move their eyelids independently is just one of their interesting characteristics. Crocodiles also can hold their breath underwater for long periods of time, thanks to the presence of a diaphragm that prevents water from entering their lungs. Additionally, they can maintain a constant body temperature through sun and shade, as well as through hot and cold water.

Crocodiles are ancient animals that have been able to survive for millions of years due to their ability to adapt to environmental changes. They are also important for wetland ecosystems as they help maintain ecological balance and serve as indicators of the health of aquatic environments.

Pangolins are the most trafficked mammals in the world

Pangolins are curious and unique animals in the world. They are the most trafficked mammals on the planet, due to their commercial value on the black market. These animals are sought after for their meat, which is considered a delicacy in some countries, but primarily for their scales that have healing properties in traditional Asian medicine.

Pangolins have an appearance like a large anteater covered in scales. They mainly live in Africa and Asia and are known for their ability to roll up into a ball when they feel threatened. Their scales are made of keratin, the same substance that makes up human nails, and are used in powdered form for traditional medicines, creating a global demand for this animal.

Hunting and trading of pangolins are illegal, but their black market continues to thrive. There are eight species of pangolins, all of them at risk of extinction due to hunting and habitat loss. International organizations like the Convention on International Trade in Endangered Species of Wild Fauna and Flora (CITES) are working to protect these precious creatures and restrict their illegal trade.

Pangolins are extraordinarily vulnerable animals, and their illegal trafficking is seriously threatening their survival. However, thanks to the joint efforts of international organizations and governments, there is hope for the protection of this unique species. It is important that we all do our part to support wildlife conservation efforts, such as for pangolins, to ensure they will continue to exist for future generations.

Deer are capable of swimming long distances

Deer are animals that primarily live on land, but not everyone knows that these elegant animals are also skilled swimmers. Although swimming is not a daily activity for them, deer can cover long distances in water, and sometimes swimming can be essential for their survival.

Deer are able to swim thanks to their long and strong legs, which allow them to move easily in water. Additionally, their slender and muscular body is perfect for swimming as it offers low water resistance.

While swimming, deer keep their heads held high above the water, propelling themselves forward with their legs. Thanks to their large antlers, which function as buoyancy aids, they are also able to maintain balance while swimming.

In nature, deer may be forced to swim across watercourses or lakes to search for food or escape from predators. Additionally, swimming can be useful for them to move from one area to another within their habitat, which may include water bodies.

Although swimming is not their preferred activity, deer are extremely versatile and adaptable animals, capable of surviving in different environments and situations. Their swimming ability is just one of the many features that make them extraordinary animals.

Hummingbirds can fly backwards thanks to their wings that move in a full arc

Hummingbirds are unique birds, known for their incredible flying abilities. But there's another skill that makes them even more special: they can fly backwards. This is a feature that no other bird possesses and allows hummingbirds to feed very efficiently.

But how do hummingbirds fly backwards? The answer lies in their ability to move their wings in a full arc, thanks to a very particular joint. This way, hummingbirds can create an air thrust that propels them forward or backward, depending on how they move their wings.

But it's not just the ability to fly backwards that makes hummingbirds so special. These birds can also fly at incredible speeds, reaching up to 50 miles per hour, thanks to their lightweight structure and fan-shaped wings that generate high lift. Moreover, hummingbirds can hover in a fixed position in the air, thanks to their amazing ability to hover by beating their wings up to 80 times per second.

In short, hummingbirds are true sky acrobats, capable of doing things that no other bird can do. And not only that: their beauty and charm also make them among the most admired and beloved birds in the world.

Cats have 32 muscles in their ears, twice as many as humans

Cats are known for their exceptional hearing ability, thanks to their incredible 32 muscles in their ears, twice as many as humans.

This allows cats to orient their ears independently and capture sounds from different directions, and to hear even very high-frequency sounds that are inaudible to humans. Additionally, cats can quickly move their ears to capture even the faintest sounds, making them skilled hunters. Some studies have shown that cats can even distinguish the sounds of different types of birds or rodents and know exactly where to look for them.

This incredible hearing ability also helps cats communicate with each other through a wide range of meows, purrs, and growling sounds.

In short, cats have a truly unique and sophisticated auditory system that helps them survive and thrive in their natural environment.

Gibbons are the fastest primates in the world

Gibbons are a group of agile and fast primates, known for their acrobatics in the trees. They are considered the fastest primates in the world, capable of moving quickly through the jungle, leaping from one tree to another at impressive speeds. Their slender and elongated bodies, combined with their long arms, make them well-suited for movement in the treetops.

Gibbons employ a form of locomotion called brachiation, which involves moving from one tree to another by grasping branches and vines with their hands. This method of movement requires great strength in the arms and shoulders, and gibbons are highly skilled in this regard. They can cover great distances in very little time, reaching speeds of over 50 km/h.

Furthermore, gibbons are also excellent jumpers. They are capable of leaping from one tree to another over distances that can exceed 10 meters. This jumping ability allows them to traverse the gaps between trees, avoiding descent to the ground where there would be predators and other dangers.

Although gibbons are the fastest primates in the world, unfortunately, they are also among the most endangered primate species. Their population has decreased drastically due to the loss of their natural habitat and indiscriminate hunting. It is important to protect these special creatures and ensure they have enough space and resources to thrive and flourish in the tropical forests they inhabit.

White rhinoceroses can weigh up to 4600 pounds

The white rhinoceros is one of the largest terrestrial mammals in existence. These sturdy and massive animals can weigh up to 4600 pounds and reach a shoulder height of approximately 6 feet. Males are generally larger than females and can have a front horn measuring up to 5.5 feet long.

White rhinos are native to southern Africa and have long been hunted for their horn, which is considered a status symbol in some Asian cultures and is used in traditional medicine. Due to hunting and habitat loss, the white rhinoceros has become an endangered species. Fortunately, thanks to conservation efforts, the white rhino population has stabilized in recent years.

The white rhinoceros is a solitary animal that prefers to graze in grassy areas near water sources. Their diet primarily consists of grass, but they can also eat shrubs and trees depending on food availability. Unlike other large animals, white rhinos are rather slow and clumsy when it comes to running, but they can still reach a top speed of about 25 miles per hour.

The white rhinoceros is an impressive animal that captivates the attention of many people. However, the conservation of this species is extremely important for maintaining the balance of African ecosystems and safeguarding the biological diversity of our planet.

Meerkats live in groups of 20-30 individuals, working together to protect their territory.

Meerkats are highly sociable animals that live in groups of 20-30 individuals, known as clans. These clans work together to protect their territory and find food. Each member of the clan has a specific role to play, with some keeping watch for predators, while others search for food or care for the young.

One of the most well-known behaviors of meerkats is their habit of standing upright on two legs, using their tail for support. This behavior is often associated with predator scanning, as it allows them to have a better view of the surrounding territory.

Meerkats are also known for their highly developed alarm system, capable of quickly alerting other clan members to the presence of potential danger. When a meerkat spots a predator, it emits a sharp call to warn the others.

Meerkats are highly adaptable and can survive in various environments, from grasslands to desert areas. Their main food consists of insects and small animals such as lizards and snakes.

Thanks to their sociable nature and their ability to protect their territory, meerkats have become a symbol of cooperation and organization within the animal community.

Spiders can produce up to seven different types of silk

Spiders are known for their ability to produce silk, but perhaps not everyone knows that they can produce up to seven different types of silk, each with a specific function. Silk is produced by the silk glands located in the spider's abdomen and can vary in texture, color, and strength.

For example, the silk used to build spider webs is very strong and has a special structure that allows it to stretch and return to its original shape without being damaged. Some spider species also produce silk to wrap their prey or build shelters.

Furthermore, some spiders produce silk that has adhesive properties, used to capture prey. Others produce silk that emits fluorescent light, used for communication among members of the same species.

The production of silk by spiders is one of nature's wonders, and its diversity and complexity demonstrate the ability of animals to adapt to the demands of their surrounding environment.

Hedgehogs can roll into a ball to protect themselves from predators

Hedgehogs are nocturnal animals belonging to the family Erinaceidae, found in Europe, Asia, and Africa. They are easily recognizable by their characteristic rounded shape and sharp spines.

One of the most well-known behaviors of hedgehogs is their ability to roll into a ball as a method of self-defense against predators. When they feel threatened, hedgehogs curl up into a ball protected by their spines, making it difficult to attack them. However, not all hedgehogs can roll into a ball: only the species of hedgehogs that live in Europe and Asia have this ability, while African hedgehogs do not.

Hedgehogs are primarily nocturnal and solitary animals, although they can share territory with other hedgehogs. Their preferred food is insects, but they also eat fruits, berries, and small animals such as lizards, mice, and birds. Hedgehogs have an average lifespan of about 4-7 years in the wild.

Hedgehogs are beneficial to the ecosystem as they feed on harmful insects like mosquitoes and ants. However, their natural habitat is increasingly threatened by urbanization and pollution, making their survival difficult. There are initiatives to protect hedgehogs, such as creating shelters and raising awareness about their importance to the ecosystem.

Koalas can sleep up to 22 hours a day.

Koalas are known to be sleepy animals, capable of sleeping up to 22 hours a day. This is because their eucalyptus leaf diet provides them with low nutritional value, so their metabolism slows down and they spend a significant amount of time sleeping and digesting.

Koalas do not sleep for 22 consecutive hours, but rather divide their sleep into several-hour sessions. Most of their time is spent resting in trees, trying to avoid excessive heat or cold.

During sleep, koalas adopt very strange positions, such as huddling on a branch or even hanging upside down. This is because their limbs are very strong and equipped with sharp claws that allow them to climb trees with ease.

Despite their adorable and sleepy appearance, koalas are very active animals during the night when they come out to search for food and socialize with other koalas in the area. Their nocturnal behavior is often accompanied by guttural sounds and cries that serve to communicate with each other and defend their territory against intruders.

Snowy owls have feathers on their feet to keep them warm in snowy conditions

The snowy owl is a nocturnal bird of prey that lives in the Arctic and subarctic regions of Europe, Asia, and North America. This bird has a soft white plumage and dark feathers that give it a spectacular and fascinating appearance. One of its most remarkable features is the presence of feathers on its feet, which help keep them warm in the cold snowy conditions.

The feathers on the feet of snowy owls are notable because they are covered with small hair-like feathers called fovea feathers. These feathers, along with the scales on their feet, allow the owl to walk on the snow without sinking, as they create a kind of air cushion under their feet that acts as thermal insulation.

Additionally, snowy owls have large yellow eyes that adapt to night vision and help them hunt during the night. They can also rotate their heads up to 270 degrees, which means they can turn their heads almost completely around their neck, allowing them to see all around them without having to move too much.

Despite their adaptation to cold climates, snowy owls are not able to survive in extreme temperatures, such as those of a polar winter. In these cases, they rely on their ability to conserve body heat by huddling up in a ball and covering themselves with their wings. This is just one of the many fascinating characteristics of this species of nocturnal birds that continue to captivate the attention of wildlife enthusiasts worldwide.

Crocodiles can live up to a hundred years

Crocodiles are some of the longest-living animals on the planet. These prehistoric reptiles can live up to a hundred years, although most of them do not reach this age due to environmental threats and human hunting.

Crocodiles are found in many parts of the world, from the swamps of Africa to the rainforests of Central and South America, to the saltwater habitats of Australia. They are known for their tough, scaly skin and their immense strength, but also for their ability to remain motionless for hours, patiently waiting for the right prey.

Crocodiles are also famous for their distinctive roar, which can be heard over long distances. Despite their reputation as ruthless predators, crocodiles are important for the ecosystem as they help control the population of other animals and play a significant role in the food chain.

However, due to habitat loss and illegal hunting for their skin and meat, many crocodile species are now at risk of extinction.

Camels have eyelids that close horizontally to protect their eyes from sand

Camels are extraordinarily adaptable animals, capable of surviving in extreme environments with few resources. One of their most interesting features is their ability to close their eyelids horizontally. This characteristic allows camels to protect their eyes from sand and sandstorms that can occur in the deserts where they live.

The upper eyelid of the camel moves horizontally to meet the lower eyelid, creating a protective slit for the eyes. In this way, camels can continue to see even in windy and sandy conditions when other animals would be blind.

Furthermore, camels also have very long and thick eyelashes that help filter sand and dust from the air they breathe. These eyelashes are so effective that they can trap even the smallest particles, ensuring good air quality reaching their lungs.

The camel's ability to adapt to the extreme conditions of the desert is an example of their incredible survival skills. Thanks to these and other unique features, camels can traverse long stretches of sand and even survive for weeks without water or food.

Lemurs are nocturnal and spend most of the day sleeping

Lemurs are nocturnal animals native to Madagascar. Their nocturnal lifestyle is due to competition with other diurnal animals inhabiting the island. Lemurs therefore spend most of the day sleeping, resting in tree cavities or on branches above their heads. During the night, they wake up and feed on leaves, fruits, and insects.

Lemurs are also known for their social behavior. They live in groups that can range from 2 to 30 individuals and are highly bonded to their family. Mothers are very protective of their offspring and often carry them wherever they go. Additionally, lemurs communicate with each other through a range of sounds and gestures including moaning, calling, and greeting.

Among the most well-known lemurs are the slender loris, the pygmy lemur, the sifaka lemur, and the ring-tailed lemur. The latter is probably the most famous lemur, thanks to its appearance in the Madagascar animated movies. The ring-tailed lemur is also known for its long, bushy tail and its black and white facial stripes.

Unfortunately, many lemur species are at risk of extinction due to habitat loss and illegal hunting. The conservation of lemurs and their forests is important not only for the survival of these animals but also for the health of the Madagascar ecosystem and the communities dependent on it.

Sea urchins have venomous spines that protect them from predators

Sea urchins are marine animals that live on rocky or sandy seabeds in all the world's oceans. They are known for their spines, which they use to defend themselves against predators. But not all sea urchin spines are the same: some of them can be venomous.

The venom produced by sea urchin spines is composed of a mixture of toxins, some of which can be dangerous to humans. The venom can cause intense pain, swelling, itching, and other symptoms. In extreme cases, it can even be lethal.

However, not all sea urchins have venomous spines, and not all sea urchin spines are venomous. Generally, larger and more colorful sea urchins have more venomous spines compared to their smaller and less conspicuous counterparts.

It is always best to avoid touching sea urchins, as even non-venomous spines can cause pain and skin irritation. If stung by a sea urchin, it is important to immediately wash the affected area with saltwater and seek medical assistance if severe symptoms occur.

Parrots can learn to repeat human phrases and words

Parrots are known for their ability to imitate human sounds and words. In fact, many species of parrots can learn and repeat phrases and words after hearing them repeatedly. Their brains are highly developed and have a learning capacity like that of primates. This ability has made parrots popular as pets, as many owners enjoy the idea of having a talking animal.

However, it is important to remember that parrots are intelligent and social animals that require constant interaction and stimulation to maintain their health and happiness. Keeping a parrot as a pet requires a lot of care and attention, as these birds are very demanding. Additionally, the decision to acquire a parrot as a pet should only be made if one is willing to take care of it for its entire lifespan, which can be decades.

Bats can eat up to 1200 insects per hour

Bats, also known as chiroptera, are nocturnal mammals that feed on insects and fruits. It is estimated that there are over 1,400 species of bats worldwide, making them one of the most diverse mammals in terms of species. Bats are known for their ability to fly and navigate in darkness using echolocation. However, their most impressive ability may be their capacity to consume large quantities of insects.

Bats can eat up to 1200 insects per hour. This makes them very important for the ecosystem as they help control the insect population and prevent the spread of insect-borne diseases. Bats can be found in a wide range of habitats, from forests to meadows, deserts, and even cities.

Not all bats feed on insects. Some species feed on fruits, pollen, nectar, or blood. However, those that feed on insects are the most common. When bats feed on insects, they capture their prey in flight using their wings and sharp teeth. They are capable of capturing insects of various sizes and types, such as mosquitoes, moths, grasshoppers, flies, and many others.

Bats play an important role in maintaining the ecosystem. By consuming a large quantity of insects, they help prevent crop destruction and maintain the natural balance of the environment. Unfortunately, some bat species are endangered due to habitat loss and hunting by humans. It is important to protect these animals and ensure that they can continue to fulfill their important role in the ecosystem.

Dogs have a sense of smell 100,000 times more sensitive than humans

The sense of smell in dogs is known to be incredibly developed and sensitive. In fact, it has been shown that dogs' olfactory capacity is up to 100,000 times more sensitive than that of humans. This is possible due to the presence of approximately 220 million olfactory receptors in their noses, compared to only 5 million present in the human nose. Additionally, dogs also have a much larger section of their brain dedicated to processing olfactory information compared to humans.

Thanks to their ability to perceive odors, dogs have been trained to perform a wide range of tasks, including detecting explosives, drugs, missing persons, and diseases. They can detect odors that humans would not be able to perceive, such as the odors of tumors or changes in blood glucose levels.

Dogs can distinguish between different odors and can also recognize specific odors of individuals and animals. They can do this thanks to the presence of pheromones, chemical substances produced by living beings to communicate with each other. Dogs can perceive the chemical substances in the urine and feces of animals, for example, to identify the presence of a specific animal in an area.

Dogs have an extraordinarily developed sense of smell that allows them to perceive odors in much greater detail than humans. Thanks to this ability, they can perform important and useful tasks for humans.

Dolphins use their sonar to communicate with each other and locate food

Dolphins are highly intelligent and social animals. One of their most astonishing characteristics is their ability to use sonar, also known as echolocation, to communicate with each other and locate food.

Sonar is a localization system based on the sounds dolphins emit through their mouths. These sounds travel through the water and when they encounter an object, they are reflected to the dolphin in the form of an echo. The dolphin can interpret these echoes and determine the position and shape of the object.

Dolphins use sonar to communicate with each other through a series of sounds and vocalizations. Each dolphin has its own unique "whistle," which functions like a name and allows dolphins to identify each other.

Furthermore, dolphins use sonar to locate food. When a dolphin emits a sound through sonar, the echo bounces off any nearby moving object, such as a fish. This enables the dolphin to pinpoint the fish's location and catch it.

The ability to use sonar is essential for dolphins' survival as it helps them locate food and avoid predators. It is also an important tool for communication among members of their community.

Sonar is a vital tool for dolphins' survival and plays a significant role in their communication and food search. The dolphins' ability to use sonar is one of the most fascinating aspects of these intelligent and social animals.

Hedgehogs can swim and cross bodies of water

Hedgehogs are animals known for their spines, but perhaps not everyone knows that they are also capable of swimming. In fact, these small mammals are skilled swimmers and can cross bodies of water to search for food or move from one place to another.

During swimming, hedgehogs keep their legs close to their body and move their feet like fins, using their tail for balance as well. Thanks to their swimming abilities, hedgehogs can even hunt fish and aquatic insects.

However, hedgehogs are not animals that spend a lot of time in the water and they must be careful not to drown. For this reason, they prefer to avoid swimming in deep waters or in rough sea conditions.

Hedgehogs can be vulnerable when swimming in open sea, where they may become prey to predators like whales. But in general, their ability to swim is a remarkable characteristic that demonstrates their great adaptability to different situations.

Butterflies have food preferences and prefer certain flowers over others

Butterflies are delicate and fascinating creatures that not only capture attention for their beauty but also for their feeding habits. Unlike humans, butterflies do not consume solid food but instead feed on sugary liquids such as flower nectar and fermented fruits. However, not all butterflies can feed from the same sources. In fact, each butterfly species has its own food preferences and prefers certain flowers over others.

For instance, Monarch butterflies, known for their annual migration between Canada and Mexico, primarily feed on nectar from Asclepias flowers. These flowers contain chemicals that help protect butterfly larvae from predators. Swallowtail butterflies, on the other hand, prefer to feed on alfalfa flowers, which have a high sugar content.

Some butterflies can detect flower pollen through their vision. Morpho butterflies, for example, feed on Banana flowers, which have a funnel shape that captures pollen. Butterflies also use their sense of smell to locate food sources. The Orange butterfly, for instance, is attracted to Asclepias flowers due to their strong scent.

Butterflies not only play an important role in plant pollination but also in the selection of the flowers they feed on. Their feeding preferences contribute to the diversity of ecosystems by helping spread pollen and maintain ecological balance.

Snails have teeth and a ribbon-like tongue, like those of tadpoles

Snails are somewhat strange and peculiar animals, but there are even more unusual things to know about them. One of these is that, despite their slow and clumsy appearance, they have a mouth equipped with 25,000 microscopic teeth and a tongue like that of tadpoles.

Experts say that these small creatures use their teeth to scratch, scrape, and eat almost any type of plant matter, from wood to fungi, and from leaves to plant roots. Furthermore, their ribbon-like tongue is lined with thousands of tiny hook-like teeth, used to grasp and hold onto food during chewing.

These teeth can also regenerate if damaged, making snails capable of feeding throughout their entire lives. However, despite this ability to eat almost anything, snails also have food preferences and prefer certain types of leaves and flowers over others. In short, snails are not only slow and clumsy, but they also have an interesting mouth and a selective palate!

Flying squirrels are able to glide for long distances thanks to the extended skin between their hind legs

Flying squirrels are among the largest mammals capable of flying, but they glide rather than fly like birds. Their ability to fly is the result of an extended skin called a patagium that stretches between their hind legs and the lower part of their body. When they jump from a tree, flying squirrels spread their wings and glide through the air for impressive distances.

The patagium is made up of a thin and resilient membrane that extends from the tips of their hind limb digits to the base of their tail. When the flying squirrel leaps from a tree, it spreads its hind legs, extends the patagium, and uses its body to maintain the trajectory of its flight. Flying squirrels can glide for distances of up to 200 feet, maintaining speeds of 35 miles per hour.

Flying squirrels are nocturnal and spend most of their time in treetops. They have sharp claws that enable them to easily climb vertical tree trunks and branches. Their diet consists primarily of fruits, leaves, flowers, and tree sap.

Although flying squirrels are common in some parts of the world, such as Asia, Europe, and North America, their survival is threatened due to habitat loss and hunting. In certain cultures, flying squirrels are considered a culinary delicacy or used as a source of traditional medicine.

Kangaroos can reproduce only when there is enough food available

Kangaroos are unique animals that live exclusively in Australia and are known for their ability to jump long distances with their powerful hind legs. But there is another distinctive feature that sets them apart: their reproduction is closely tied to the availability of food.

In practice, female kangaroos can only reproduce when there is enough food to support pregnancy and the nursing of their young. If food resources are scarce, females can delay pregnancy or even abort if already pregnant.

This ability to regulate reproduction based on available resources is known as "short delayed implantation" and is an evolutionary adaptation that helps kangaroos survive during periods of food scarcity. Additionally, female kangaroos can produce highly nutritious milk that allows their young to grow rapidly and become independent as early as possible.

Kangaroos are highly adaptable animals that can adjust their reproduction according to food availability. This adaptive capability is one of the reasons why kangaroos have been able to survive in Australia for such a long time, despite the challenging climate and environmental conditions of the continent.

Lions can sleep for up to 20 hours a day.

Lions are known for their strength and agility, but also for their rest. In fact, these large felines can sleep for up to 20 hours a day! This may seem surprising, but it is due to their nature as carnivorous animals. Lions spend most of their time resting and digesting the food they have consumed, which can often be plentiful.

Furthermore, lions are social animals that live in groups called prides, where there is a well-defined hierarchy and division of labor. Adult males, known as "lions," are generally responsible for protecting the territory and females, while females, called "lionesses," oversee hunting and raising the cubs.

Rest is crucial for maintaining balance within the pride, as each member has an important role to play. Additionally, sleeping helps lions conserve energy and maintain a constant body temperature, especially during the hottest hours of the day.

Despite their extended rest, lions are still very active and agile when it comes to hunting prey. With their strength and hunting skills, lions can bring down animals much larger than themselves. This demonstrates that even though they may appear lazy, lions are formidable animals equipped with tremendous energy when needed.

Animals can have different personalities and behaviors even within the same species

While animals are often thought of as beings with standardized and predictable behaviors, the reality is quite different. In fact, animals can exhibit different personalities and behaviors, just like humans.

Some research has shown that, for example, mice have different personalities and that these traits influence their behavior, food choices, and how they interact with other individuals of the same species.

Even among primates, individual differences can be observed in terms of sociability, propensity for cooperation, and levels of aggression.

But it's not just that: even among domesticated animals, such as dogs, different personalities can be found, influenced by genetic, environmental, and life experiences factors.

These behavioral diversities extend not only to individual animals but also to interactions between members of the same species. For example, elephants recognize each other and can form friendships and alliances with other members of their community.

Animals are not simple and stereotyped creatures; they exhibit a great behavioral diversity
that makes each individual unique and irre-
placeable.

Conclusion: The importance of knowing and respecting animals

In this final chapter, we want to emphasize the importance of understanding and respecting the animals with whom we share the planet. Beyond the curiosities and wonders we have explored in this book; we must also consider the responsibility we have as human beings to protect and preserve animal life.

Gaining a better understanding of animals helps us comprehend their significance in our ecosystem and the role they play in the food chain. It also helps us develop a sense of empathy and respect for these living beings, which, in turn, can enhance our quality of life.

We must also consider how our daily actions, such as the use of animal-derived products or pollution, can negatively impact animal life and the environment they inhabit. It is, therefore, important that each of us does our part to reduce the negative impact our actions can have on the environment and animals.

Knowledge of animals is not only intriguing but can also have a significant impact on our lives and our environment. We must be aware of the role we can play in protecting animal life and act accordingly to preserve and safeguard the fauna of our planet.